Turning Point

Mansukh Patel and Anita Goswami

lfp

First published in the United Kingdom in 1999 by
Life Foundation Publications, Maristowe House,
Dover Street, Bilston,
West Midlands, WV14 6AL

ISBN 1 87360615 X

Printed by Biddles Ltd, Woodbridge Park Estate,
Woodbridge Road, Guildford, Surrey GU1 1DA

Dedication

To all of you who have allowed
your personal turning points
to become an inspiration
in the lives of others

Contents

Acknowledgements

A book is never created solely through the efforts of its authors. Without the energy and support and skills of many dedicated friends and colleagues it could not come into being. This book is, in many ways, a culmination of the life experiences of all the people who have contributed to it. Our main debt of gratitude goes to all those dear friends of ours who have been so open and generous in sharing their true life stories which appear in this book – Michael Shealy, Bertram van Alphen, Jean, Sally Meadows, Andrew Longman, Derek Budge, Jeanne Katz, Corien de Witte, Moon Rahman, Natasha Worrall, Joan Groves, Barbara Worrall and Sheila Roberts as well as those others who have preferred to remain anonymous. Their experiences and challenges are offered as their gift to your life. Our heartfelt thanks also go to Sally Langford and Kate Couldwell for their love, insights and enthusiasm in compiling these stories and editing the text, to Barbara Wood for her joyful dedication and creativity in graphic design and Gordon Turner for his constant support. We would also like to thank Paul Gray of Abbey Studios and Philip Engelen for the use of their photographs, and the proofreaders, Margaret Nicholas, Boris Worrall, Sally Longman, Ruth Boaler and Shona Sutherland for their patience and clarity.

How to use this book

We would like to suggest a few simple points that will help you to get the maximum benefit from this book. Each Turning Point Technique has the potential to create all the changes you might wish for but there are certain factors that are essential to understand if you are to make them really effective.

We advise you to:

♦ not rush through the stories, but rather take time to savour them.

♦ not to watch TV at the same time!

♦ take time to record any creative thoughts that may come up on the pages provided.

♦ just stay with whatever emotions may emerge while you are reading. Process them gently and allow them to be transformed.

And the techniques:

♦ sincere repetition will make them work for you.

♦ it's important to do them mindfully and with full awareness.

♦ do not be in a hurry to share the benefits you experience with anyone before they have had a chance to settle inside you. Work with them for a while first.

♦ they need your participation! Just start one and do it every day.

Introduction

Life is a series of turning points. Sometimes they are major events that dramatically alter the course of our lives, but often they can be small, seemingly insignificant moments in time that nevertheless move us into another gear or a new direction. Whether they are aware of it or not, everyone whose life has become even slightly mundane is secretly looking for a turning point, simply because no-one really wants to continue to exist in monotony. It is often difficult, however, to know how to move out of one way of being and into another.

What many people do not realise is that all 'stuck' places in life are mirror reflections of where we have become stuck in our thinking and attitudes. All our experiences are essentially a state of mind and turning points have a way of jolting us out of one mind-set and into a new way of looking at and experiencing the way we are choosing to live our life.They bring in fresh energy that clears away the debris of old, outmoded ways of being, just like a rush of clear, clean water into a stagnant pool. Sometimes they happen when we least expect them, or we are simply unaware that we are stuck, and other times they present themselves to us disguised as challenges.

If you are feeling stuck in your life – and even if you are not - this book will stimulate your heart and stir the imagination as it is full of the most enriching and dramatic real life stories. There is nothing more fascinating than the experiences and happenings of other people's lives and they hold the potential to completely redirect our own lives in the most amazing way.

Each turning point invites us to engage in life's intricate dance, but we need to be willing to participate in the process. Our recent visits to South Africa and the Sudan, the Balkans and Bangladesh have confirmed for us that it is the power that is unleashed from within the cutting edge of life's rawest experiences that leads us on to discover our own unique purpose in life. We never need feel that we are alone or too small in this universe once we realise we are in the company of such people as those who have shared their experiences in this book. Everybody's story has the potential to inspire someone to keep reaching towards their highest destiny.

At the very least, these stories and techniques will bring you to a place inside yourself where you can appreciate the wonder of your life. Perhaps Blake was experiencing this when he wrote,

> 'To see the world in a grain of sand
> and heaven in a flower,
> hold infinity in the palm of your hand
> and eternity in an hour…..'

At the very most they will catalyse the turning point you have been waiting for.

The same stream of life
that runs through my veins night and day
runs through the world and dances
in rhythmic measures.
It is the same life that shoots in joy
through the dust of the earth
in numberless blades of grass
and breaks into tumultuous waves
of leaves and flowers.
It is the same life that is rocked in the ocean cradle
of birth and death in ebb and in flow.
I feel my limbs are made glorious
by the touch of this world of life
and my pride is from the life throb of ages
dancing in my blood at this moment.

Rabindranath Tagore

See the
synchronicity

'Learn to sit at the feet of your own life
and be taught by it.'

P. Berrien Berends

TURNING POINT - MANSUKH

*T*he circumstances were not an obvious backdrop for a miracle to happen - a disused cemetery in the middle of St. Petersburg on a bleak, drizzly day, next to a death wall, still pitted with hundreds of bullet holes where eighty monks had been shot to death seventy years before. An old woman dressed in black shuffled around the cemetery, sweeping leaves from the graves with her broom, while beggars lined the streets outside. An atmosphere of hopelessness and despair pervaded the impoverished city.

But out of this great darkness a radiance of hope was to emerge and enter the moment in such a way as to change the direction of my life.

We thought we were there as part of our Eurowalk Russian tour to interview one of the more outspoken orthodox priests who had a far-reaching vision for the church. We were also there to find ways to help heal the wounds of the people in war-torn Chechnya. While we were talking I noticed the old woman moving silently around the tombstones. There was something about her, I didn't know what, that compelled me to break the pre-arranged interview to talk to her. I moved towards her, and in response to my greeting she smiled and nodded, making an unusual sound with her throat. I suddenly realised she was mute. Later on I discovered she had lost her voice through illness as a young woman some fifty years before. Because she couldn't speak she communicated to the world through her eyes, the tips of her fingers and via a little notepad and pencil which she pulled out of the many layers of ragged clothing she wore.

Through her beautifully formed handwriting I discovered her name was Alexandria and when I told her mine, she looked up at me and gently touched my face with her old wrinkled hand. Her soft, kind eyes looked straight into mine in such a way that I was instantly reminded of my own dear mother. The gesture was a tender one and her gaze penetrating and ancient. The dark and gloomy cemetery had suddenly turned into an enchanted garden.

And in that moment I knew that this was one of those magical gifts from the universe; a moment in time arranged by a much higher intelligence for my personal benefit.

'You must pray to the Mother.' She scratched out her message and pointed to the wall where a picture of Mother Mary was perched between the bullet holes. I looked back at the babushka* and asked the priest to ask her if she meant I should pray in the morning or evening.

'Always,' came the scribbled reply and all at once it felt as though the dazzling lights of the Aurora Borealis were illuminating the night sky as the atmosphere became alive and electrified by her message. 'Always'.

* Russian wise woman

TURNING POINT - MANSUKH

Have you ever felt that God was talking directly to you through someone else? In that moment I felt myself being dragged into an energy that I simply could not resist. It completely engulfed me, at the same time catapulting me into a realisation about my greater purpose in life.

I found myself understanding what Gandhi meant when he said, 'There comes a time when an individual becomes all-pervasive in his effect. This comes when he reduces himself to zero.'

Something opened up inside me and I was suddenly flowing in the same stream, fully awake to what I had to do next. From that moment on my life has moved into another gear entirely. Something has matured inside me and a greater depth of understanding, compassion and courage has emerged. Prayer, for me, is no longer an act that is somehow separate from life. It is a living act within the everyday happenings and joys of life.

Mansukh

'The same stream of life that runs through my veins night and day runs through the world and dances in rhythmic measures.'

Rabindranath Tagore

There is a beautiful synchronicity in the universe that causes everything to move and interact with everything else from the exploding supernova in a distant galaxy to the movement of earthworms under your feet. This exquisite dance of creation is something we can consciously choose to ignore or to fully participate in. But whatever we do, miracles are happening all around us all the time. The question is, where are we? If we are too busy or the mind is moving too fast, we can completely miss the magic of the moment.

In my tradition it is generally accepted that the connection between us is a very real and tangible one. As Herman Melville, the American novelist and poet, once said, 'a thousand fibres connect us with our fellow men'. We all breathe the same air and that air has been breathed in by millions of others throughout the ages, including people like Jesus and Krishna. If the air I breathe is changed by its contact with my body, mind and consciousness how will it affect the living being next to me who breathes it in? Because we take in tiny light particles of each other's personality and emotions all the time it is perfectly feasible that we may be breathing in molecules of great people like Jesus, Michelangelo or Gandhi. Just consider for a moment that you may have cells from Christ's heart inside your body, or a brain cell from Einstein. It's a fascinating thought, isn't it?

When I meet someone like Alexandria, who reminds me so much of my mother, I am totally open to the possibility that there really is an intrinsic aspect of my mother standing in front of me, sent to infuse me and guide me forward. We are all participating in the synchronicity of life, but failing to recognise this, we may miss the most poignant messages that life is trying to communicate to us.

If you have ever met someone who ignited something so powerful within you that it changed the course of your life you will understand what I mean. And I truly believe that it is possible to open oneself up to an unimpeded flow of divine intelligence throughout every moment of the day. This means that every encounter becomes a potentially impactful one, and life itself an almighty expression of healing - out of ignorance and into wisdom. Each moment then becomes totally full and complete. This experience of wholeness is described in a prayer I have used every day since I was a child:

'This is fullness, that is fullness, everything is fullness. Fullness brings forth fullness. When fullness is taken away from fullness, fullness remains.'

The Upanishads

Q If you suddenly discovered that you really did have cells from Jesus in your body, what difference would it make to the way you live your life?

Q How meaningful are your interactions with people? Give yourself marks out of ten.

Q How can you make your interactions more meaningful?

Turning

Point techniques

- Stand back and contemplate the synchronicity of events for a moment and consider who may be standing right in front of you.

- Ask yourself what meaning they may be holding for you personally. This can open up a magical universe in which you will never, ever be without a friend to guide and help you. This means you will never feel lonely again.

- You can only 'see the synchronicity' through a right brain state of awareness. Practise developing the right side of your brain by 'being' more than 'doing'. For example:

- Develop an appreciation, gratitude, wonderment and excitement about yourself and the world around you.

- Each day walk barefoot on the grass. Touch a leaf and stand still without moving.
  Listen to a bird singing for at least thirty seconds *with all your attention.*

- Write a poem or song - even if it's only two lines!

- Once a month sleep outside.

- Smell flowers!

- Be creative. Start painting, drawing, singing and writing. Whatever appeals to you, become so absorbed in it that the world just passes you by.

- Really listen to music rather than blanking it out, and observe how you feel.

Your notes

Follow
your destiny

'I don't know what your destiny will be, but one thing I know; the only ones among you who will be really happy are those who have sought and found how to serve.'

Albert Schweitzer

'*D*o you see that star, Anita?' My grandfather's voice was kind and loving, at the same time tinged with mystery. I was sitting on his lap, as I often did as a child, outside in the courtyard of our house in Kampala. I looked up at the star which stood apart from all the others, nodding enthusiastically and waited for him to explain. 'That is the North Star,' he said, 'known in our tradition as Dru'.

'Dru?' I asked, immediately intrigued.

'Dru is an Indian word meaning 'Pole Star', he explained, 'and many years ago, when I was a young man living in India, a great teacher came to our village and explained to me that if you want to gain stability and a better understanding of life, it is very auspicious to meditate on the Dru Star.' I closed my eyes and tried to imagine my grandfather as a young man, standing alone under the deep night sky, appealing to the North Star for guidance. 'Is that why you sit here every evening?' I asked him. 'Under the stars?' He nodded knowingly.

'And I always pray that everyone in our family will find what they have come here for,' he said softly. His words were weaving a magical atmosphere around me as he spoke, creating a very special feeling - a feeling which, unbeknown to me at that time, was to embed itself deeply into my heart for the rest of my life. I leaned closer to him, instinctively warming to his love for us, my young heart full of gratitude for his presence in our lives.

Kampala, holds many soft, warm memories for me. The endless days of my childhood were carefree and happy, surrounded as we were by love and financial security. I remember endless summer evenings running through the long grass that rustled in the breeze. It seemed to me that the breath-taking spaces went on for ever, interrupted only by the seven hills of Kampala. At night my twin sister and I lay listening to crickets, giant croaking toads and the occasional cry of an exotic bird.

When I was in my early teens, this idyllic atmosphere began to change as I became aware of a growing feeling of mistrust and insecurity felt by the Asian communities in Uganda. Africanisation policies were being introduced, creating potential difficulties for my father, who worked in the world of finance. At election time I remember feeling a chill running through my spine when I heard gunshots coming from the local stadium. We lived only three doors away from Idi Amin and when we looked out to see tanks parked on the pavement outside his house, it was very obvious that something was wrong. One day my father received a tip-off from the CID chief in Kampala, who was a close personal friend. 'Things are going to get tough,' he said urgently. 'If I were you I would get out while the going is good.' Quickly my father took steps to set all his affairs in order so that everything would be all right for a few months while he was away settling us all in England. He never did return to continue his business however, because within six months the coup had taken place and all Asians had been forcibly expelled from Uganda.

Life in England presented many challenges at first. Not only did we have to adapt to a completely new and strange way of life in an unknown country, but we were split up as a family for six months until my father could find somewhere big enough for us all to live together. We also had the rather traumatic experience of visiting friends or relatives who had not been as fortunate as we had. They had to leave everything behind in Uganda as they fled to the stations and airports, not even knowing if they would be granted safe passage. Arriving in Britain they were living in camps until more permanent accommodation could be found for them.

As I struggled to prove myself in my adopted country I gradually lost sight of the indigenous wisdom I had been brought up with. Pressure from peer groups, the stress of exams, the need to be seen to be successful and the lure of material trappings all led me away from the values of trust, inner peace and contentment that had nourished my childhood years. And I paid a high price for it. By the time I reached my thirties all the magic had long gone out of my life, leaving me feeling trapped, empty, lonely and completely confused. In desperation, I looked around for someone who could help and guide me.

There was my dear mother, a very humble and compassionate soul with an unconditional acceptance and love for humanity. She has always believed that whatever happens in life is meant to be and is all part of the divine plan. 'There's no point in getting upset about what's going on,' she would say to me. 'It's much better to accept the situation as it is and to rise to meet the occasion with dignity and honour.' She really helped me reconnect with the values I had once known and lived by. And there was grandfather, of course, so full of wisdom and love. Although a simple being, he carried the presence of someone who understood life's many complexities. Was it his meditation that gave him these qualities I wondered?

My twin sister, Rita, had already been meditating and practising something called 'Dru Yoga' for many years. I had never taken too much notice when she had talked about how much it had helped her, preoccupied as I was with my own worldly pursuits. Now I began to wonder .... she certainly was very stable and content within herself and her life was totally dedicated to helping other people....Dru Yoga. What did that mean? And then it hit me. The Dru Star! That was the star my grandfather had been praying to all those years before! And then I remembered that magical evening all those years ago as I sat in my grandfather's lap under the stars. A rush of feeling came over me as I recalled his words, 'I always pray to the North Star that all of us will find what we have come here for.' Could it be that Dru Yoga held the key to my destiny and that of my sister? Was there a connection?

Who knows what the effects of one, heartfelt prayer can be, not only for ourselves, but for the lives of our loved ones and even generations to come. It was just too much of a co-incidence to ignore and I simply had to investigate further. Rita introduced me to five leading Dru yoga exponents, one of whom was Mansukh. I also met his wife Jane, as well as the now well-known Annie Jones, John Jones and Chris Barrington. Through them I had the great privilege of meeting two beautiful old indigenous people who turned out to be the 'keepers of the keys' of Dru yoga - Mansukh's parents. They were the people who really connected me to the power of the Dru Star and from that moment on my life turned around completely. I started to meditate and to practise yoga and immediately began to feel healthier and more alive than ever before. But not only that, I felt a force of inner strength beginning to rise up inside me, propelling me forward to seek new and more meaningful horizons. I felt re-connected once again to the stillness and certainty I had once known as a child. It wasn't long before I felt compelled to take my new-found freedom out into the world to teach others the skills and methods that had enabled me to find myself.

Anita

'I have no shadow of a doubt that any man or woman can achieve what I have, if he or she would make the same effort and cultivate the same hope and faith.'

Mahatma Gandhi

The story of Dru is now, understandably, very close to my heart. My tradition is very rich in stories of the lives of great beings. They portray deep, eternal truths in an easily understandable form. Dru's story is one such example and has been a great source of inspiration to me over the years.

Dru, or Druvam was the son of a great and noble King called Uttanapada, who had two wives, Suniti and Suruchi. Druvam – or Dru – was Suniti's son and Uttama was Suruchi's son. One day when Uttama was sitting on his father's lap, Dru came to climb up as well, but Uttama's mother, who was very jealous of Dru, rushed over to pull him away from the king. 'You will never be good enough to sit on your father's lap!' she scolded. Because the king loved Suruchi very dearly his infatuation prevented him from saying anything. Dru felt so hurt and rejected that he rushed out to find his mother who took him on her lap and softly asked him not to be angry with his father. 'Always remember that you have a much greater father who will never, ever let you down. Pray to Lord Narayana and he will heal your pain. He is the greatest refuge of all.'

Dru ran out of the palace and into the forest to search for this father who would never let him down or hurt him. Although still only five years old, he meditated and prayed constantly to the Lord, begging Him to appear to him. In his desperation he ate very little for the first two months and then fasted on only water. His practice was so intense in fact, that the Lord's heart was deeply moved. He finally appeared to him in a vision and asked him what it was he wanted so much that it drove him to make such severe sacrifices.

'Give me a place in this world that is immovable,' he said to the Lord, 'a place that no-one can take away.' The Lord promised him that he would one day occupy a place that is above everyone except the Lord himself. 'All the other stars and planets will revolve around it in the heavens, but you will always remain constant.' He said. 'But first you must go back home because you are destined to rule your father's kingdom.'

Dru returned to the palace where his father welcomed him with tears of love and joy. Years later Dru did indeed become a great king and ruled his kingdom with wisdom and justice. It is said that when the time came for him to depart from this earth, the Lord sent his servants to meet him in a shining chariot. 'Many years ago Lord Narayana granted you a place in the heavens,' they said. 'We have come now to take you there.' And so Dru stepped into the chariot and was taken to his permanent abode – the North Star.

Dru's story represents our search for that immovable place within us all – the place where we are able to remain calm and still, no matter what else might be going on around us. It is a place we all long for and this point of stillness is the gift that Dru Yoga offers. As I persisted with my own yoga and meditation practice I began to understand the real significance of Dru's story. The deeper my practice became, the stiller I became within myself, although my challenges didn't suddenly disappear overnight. In fact, they often appeared to increase! But the difference was that I was able to take them in my stride and was no longer thrown off balance by them. Like Dru, we all have a much higher destiny than we are aware of, and that destiny is always calling us forward. Very often it is the most confusing and distressing moments that redirect us towards what we have really come here to do. This was certainly the case for me.

My life is so extraordinary now that it is difficult to relate to the place I had arrived at all those years ago. But there is no doubt in my mind that it was all perfect. My own destiny has unfolded in such a way that I am now travelling all over the world teaching other people how to find their own Dru Star. It is a journey that is as exciting and exhilarating as it is rewarding.

Whilst I was teaching in Australia recently, a young girl came up to me and said, 'Mummy said you work in war zones. What is a war zone?' I tried to explain to her that it is an area in the world where there is poverty and hunger, greed and violence, where people are abused or where the land and its resources are being destroyed on a massive scale. She looked puzzled. 'Why?' she asked with big, wide eyes that couldn't understand. I had to stop and ask myself that question. Why?

'War originates within us first of all,' I told her, 'and when we are at war with ourselves we cannot talk, walk or live in peace with others.' I thought about it more deeply later on and realised that the greatest lesson we all have to learn is *to make peace with ourselves.* We each have to find that point of stability within ourselves and stay there, fixed and immovable like Dru, so that nothing and no-one can shake our peace. When we cease to be at war with ourselves, peace outside ourselves will follow naturally.

Q Do you turn to the wisest or the nearest person to guide you towards your destiny?

Q Can you think of any values that were an important part of your life when you were a child and which you have now lost touch with? Would you benefit if you could incorporate them into your life again? How could you do this?

Q What is the greatest obstacle to happiness in your life?

Q Who do you regard as being your main mentor? What particular strength does this person possess?

Point techniques

- Whenever you meet people, question them about their life and what has made it successful. You may learn something that could open up your whole destiny in an entirely new way.

- Silently affirm to yourself as often as you can, 'I am travelling towards my highest destiny.'

The following two techniques will help bring calmness and stability into your life and anchor you to that place of inner stillness represented by Dru:

- Stand with your left foot firmly on the ground. Your right foot is at right angles to the left with the heel resting on the left toes. As you inhale, raise your arms above your head till the palms touch, and soften your knees. Breathe out as you straighten your knees and push your heels down into the ground. Hold for a while, breathing normally.* Lower your hands as you exhale and repeat on the other side.

- Sit down quietly with your eyes closed and allow
  your body to relax. Concentrate on your
  breathing for a while to relax your mind.
  Visualise a six pointed star behind your closed
  eyes and hold the image for as long as you can.
  When you are ready, open your eyes slowly and
  gaze at the floor for a few moments.

Do not hold you hands above your head for long if you have a heart condition.

Your notes

Live your dream

'Shoot for the moon. Even if you miss it, you will land among the stars.'

Les Brown

TURNING POINT - MICHAEL

'Your son has been drowned in an accident....' The words cut into my mind like a razor. No response. Couldn't register. The words 'your son' brought the image of his fresh young face into my awareness. That broad smile and those electric eyes... But 'has been drowned' brought no response. No point of reference, just numb disbelief.

It took quite a few months for the reality of his death to sink in and during that time I drifted through my days in a fog of non-comprehension and non-believing. Slowly but surely, the numb feelings began to turn into raw, unadulterated pain that came and went in waves that tore at my heart. But somewhere in the back of my mind I had always known he would die young. He was only twenty-six, but he had been a wild boy and had lived too close to the edge for too long...

But nothing could have prepared me for the news of my younger brother's death only six months later. He was a lighting man for motion pictures and during shooting he always used to sit on the barrel-sized high voltage transformers. We worked out that the electro-magnetic fields had probably been affecting him for some time without his knowing. He died from leukaemia aged only forty. He was right in the middle of his life, happily married with three beautiful daughters still growing up. It hit me like a train. I just couldn't understand how he could find himself so unexpectedly at the end of his young life. I was being faced with my own mortality.

The pain catapulted me out of my living reality and into a new, unknown place where I could suddenly see everything very clearly. Driving back home alone after his funeral in California, I had a long time to think in between the tears and intermittent stabs of pain that clutched at my chest. Like a contorted butterfly desperately trying to break free from the confines of its chrysalis, I struggled within myself to break out of my old, constricting identity and lifestyle. 'Life is too short,' the voice in my head was screaming, 'too precious to waste!'

I had been feeling trapped in an uninspiring job as a design engineer for the defence industry for some time. There was no place for me to excel. I had tolerated the forced mediocrity that never would allow more than average achievements simply because I needed the money. I had never dared to ask myself what I was doing there, but now it was suddenly crystal clear to me that I was wasting my life. I needed something to challenge my abilities.

By the time I reached Colorado I had made up my mind. I was getting out. I had to start using my life to the fullest and not waste another moment in compromise and postponement of fulfilling my dreams. Long before my brother died, I had dreamed of building my own house. I had looked at the possibility of a dome construction before discovering another unique concept using tyres and aluminium cans. This was something that would really stretch me but I knew I could do it. It was a personal challenge. I had neatly tucked my dream away into the closet of tomorrow, and tomorrow had just come. I gave up my job and comfortable house and walked out with only my dream in my pocket and determination in my heart.

So I started living my dream - and for the past nine years my days have never felt fuller, more contented or fulfilled. My ever supportive wife Marlice and I breed llamas and goats on our five acres of forest land. We lead sacred walks with the llamas and take time to watch the sun rise and set over the Colorado mountains. Slowly and surely I am building the house of my dreams. It is part buried under the ground and, like a cave, remains at a constant temperature summer and winter. A passive solar house with no electrical pumps, it gains heat through the windows and stores it in the house. I now feel I am honouring Mother Earth in my doing with life, not exploiting or robbing her, but turning trash into something that will draw little and give back a lot.

Ten years ago you would never have been able to convince me that I would be milking goats every morning, let alone looking after thirty llamas. We never buy any dairy products now, making our own cheese, yogurt and butter from the goats' milk which we sell locally. I have also unexpectedly become a design consultant for other people who want to build ecological houses and all this has grown from just wanting to do something with our lives that is fulfilling and worthwhile. It may not be everyone's idea of heaven, but it sure is mine.

'Life is either a daring adventure - or nothing.'

Helen Keller

Do you have a dream for your life? If you don't, you will just be letting life happen to you, taking everything as it comes and therefore existing mechanically. When you dare to have a vision however, you start to discover a vast reservoir of deep inner resources that you never even knew you had. They rise up from deep inside, like a whale surfacing for air, to meet the occasion. These resources will always match the demands of your dream.

Are you constantly making excuses as to why you cannot come alive and burn with passion? Have you learned to tone yourself down to an 'acceptable' level that fits in with your idea of what everyone else is doing? Perhaps you are feeling that although you have achieved many things you set out to do, there is still something missing? You may feel empty, unfulfilled, knowing you have not yet touched your highest potential.

The people who stand out in life are those who have dared to become passionate about their dream and decided to live it out to the full. Why not become one of those people? I heard a great story about a man called Jack who had a dream to make the world beautiful. As a landscape gardener all his time was spent in creating new and exciting ideas to bring his dream to fruition. When his doctor told him one day that he had a very serious form of cancer that required immediate surgery, he just looked at him in amazement. 'But it's springtime!' he said. 'I'm right in the middle of my planting! The operation will have to wait a few weeks.' Nothing anyone could say would dissuade him. 'I'd rather die leaving a beautiful world behind me,' he explained, 'than not be able to fulfil my dream.'

His dream was so selfless that it carried him beyond the boundaries of his bodily limitations. After planting time was over he had the operation, during which the surgeon discovered evidence of more cancer in his body. He refused all chemotherapy and radiation treatment because he felt it would interfere with his dream. Years later, and well into his eighties, Jack was still working full time, completely absorbed in fulfilling his life's dream to make the world beautiful.

Q Are you doing what you really want to do with your life?

Q If you were to die today would you be happy with your accomplishments? Would you feel fulfilled by what you have done with your life?

Q What is it costing you to ignore your vision in life?

Turning

Point techniques

We all have a dream, even if it's only tucked away somewhere deep down inside us. If you haven't discovered yours yet, try this technique to bring it to the surface.

- Imagine you are packing everything you own before moving away to the other side of the world. You are not likely to see any of your friends again and have invited them to your leaving party.

  What would you like them to say about you as a person?
  What would you like them to say that you had done?
  What would you like your family to say?
  Your best friend?
  Someone from work?
  A local charity organisation?

◆   Write down your answers to these questions. They will
    help you define what you hope to achieve in your life.
    Dreams don't usually manifest by themselves, they
    need your help. Write down all the simple steps you
    will have to take - include all the little details too -
    and a provisional time scale for achieving each
    exciting stage.

As Gandhi once said, 'full effort is full victory!'

Your notes

Make contact
with others

'We may all have come on different
ships, but we're all in the same boat now.'
M L King Jnr

*W*hy doesn't anyone look at anyone else on the subway? How can so many people be confined together in one space and never even catch each other's eyes let alone, God forbid, strike up a conversation? Have we, as a species, really become so estranged from one another? I had just read an amazing story about a man who had decided one morning to change all this. No matter what happened that morning, when he got on the train he was going to make an effort to connect with at least one other human being. That one decision changed his life and the lives of two other people.

He started with the old man sitting next to him. Breaking through his inbred natural reserve, he asked the old man about his life and discovered he had a really interesting past. He was Polish and had been in a concentration camp during the war, during which time he became separated from his wife and every other member of his family. After his release, he was told his wife and family had all died and, in an effort to forget everything and start again he had come to New York. He casually asked the old man what his wife's name was and was surprised by the fact that he knew a Polish woman of the same name. After further investigation it began to appear that this could be the same woman. But that couldn't possibly be. Or could it? 'Tell me more about your wife,' he urged him. By the time they got to their station, the man knew that it was the same woman and was so excited he could hardly contain himself. 'Wait!' he said as the Polish man turned to go, 'there's someone you must talk to!' He hauled him to the nearest call box and rang her number. Mercifully she answered. He spoke to her for a few moments before handing the phone to her husband whom she had not seen for over forty years, presuming him dead also. Can you imagine the look on his face when he heard his wife's voice on the other end of the phone?

I had to make a train journey myself just after I had read this story so I decided to follow the example. Due to an accident my train had been delayed, along with several others, so I sat down to wait and look for the person I was going to connect with. I didn't have to look far. He was sitting right next to me – a young boy of about fourteen, trembling from head to foot, visibly afraid of something. 'Are you all right?' I asked him. He jumped at my voice, looking at me suspiciously. 'I'm going to miss my Dad with this delay,' he said falteringly. 'He'll have gone by the time I get there.' And then it all came out. His parents were separated and he was going to stay with his father who would be waiting for him at the station. He couldn't reach either his father or his step-mother on the phone to tell them he would be late. My heart went out to this young boy who told me that he had just been in hospital for brain surgery. He showed me the scar on his head, stretching half way across his skull. He was as white as a sheet and I realised that a lot of his trembling was due to post-operative shock. 'What are you afraid of?' I asked him. He explained that he had just seen a programme on television showing how young boys had been kidnapped from Waterloo station where he had to wait for his father. 'What if you were to take a taxi and go straight to your father's house?' I asked. He didn't have any money. That was easy. I gave him enough money to get home as well as my name and address (he wouldn't accept the money unless he felt he could pay me back). For the first time he relaxed and smiled. After that we went our separate ways. A few days later I received a cheque and a letter from his father thanking me for looking after his son. 'You have changed my life,' it read, 'because you have restored my faith in humanity.'

What will happen in all our lives, every day, if we just take the time to break out of our own little shells and connect with our fellow human beings? Miracles.

'Love isn't something you get, but rather something you feel
when you give it to others.'

Echhaben Patel*

In a culture where loneliness and depression have reached
epidemic proportions and anti-depressants are the most widely
prescribed drugs in the world, we each have to ask ourselves why
this is so and what our part in it is. Although we are social creatures
by nature, there has been a radical shift in our social structure over
the last few years. This has meant that loneliness and isolation have
now replaced the deep sense of community and connection to
others, that we used to have. What is it in us that wants to create
walls and barriers that shut other people out?

In the high school tragedy in Littleton, Colorado, where two
seventeen year old high school students inflicted a campaign of
terror against their classmates, killing fifteen of them including
themselves, it transpired that they were part of a group of 'outcasts' -
young people who felt ostracized and rejected by their peers. The
massacre was an act of revenge against the people who had 'been
mean to them'. It turned the high school into a war zone, a small
reflection of the horror of Kosovo which had already been taking the
lives of hundreds of people for some weeks previously.

* Mansukh's mother

War reflects the inability of people like ourselves to break down the barriers that separate us from our fellow human beings. At the root of all wars lies this tendency for people to cut themselves off from each other - for whatever reason, be it race, religion, personality or just privacy. Horrors like Littleton High School are telling us that we cannot afford to allow ourselves always to retreat behind our self-imposed walls to protect ourselves from each other or to reject and exclude people from our individual sphere. In other words, we as individuals need to come out of ourselves on a daily basis and connect with the people around us. We need to make an effort to make people feel loved and appreciated and that they belong and are welcome in our world.

Mother Teresa said on many occasions that everyone was born to love and to be loved. It is our human birthright and no-one deserves to feel unloved and unwanted in life. She also said that the poverty she had seen in the incredibly lonely, isolated, unloved and uncared for people of our society far surpassed anything she had witnessed in the slums of Calcutta. This is such a sad legacy to leave our children and we are the only ones who can change it. The ground-breaking heart surgeon, Dean Ornish, has said that although heart disease is a major epidemic in America, the sense of loneliness and isolation people feel is a much greater cause of illness and disease. His research has also shown that lonely people

have a 300-500% increased risk of death from heart disease
compared to those who have a sense of love, intimacy and
connection in their lives. Walling yourself off, he says, affects and
endangers the heart, so learning to connect with others could
actually save your life.

Q How do you shut people out?

Q What kind of barriers do you create around you to protect
yourself?

Q Do you only allow certain people to get to know you and
exclude others? Who do you allow in and who do you shut out?

- Truly appreciate and honour people when you are with them. This will develop trust between you.

- Offer to do some voluntary work in your local community and you will discover the joy that comes when someone says 'thank you' and really means it. Studies show that people who do voluntary work regularly tend to be healthier and happier than those who don't.

- Project an attitude of friendship and compassion. Make sure you always include a smile, 'Hello! Good morning!' Or you could just hum a tune.

- Make a decision to say something inspiring to somebody on the way to work today.

- Decide to make contact with at least one person every day. It could be on the tube, bus or train. Or perhaps someone in the park, at a bus stop or in the supermarket queue. Even smiling at someone can make a difference to their whole day. Whatever you do, don't just ignore everyone! If you strike up a conversation, remember the story you have just read and how much one conversation can affect another person's life. In other words, never underestimate the power you have.

Your notes

Do it now!

'If you bring forth what is inside you, what you bring forth will save you. It you do not bring forth what is inside you, what you do not bring forth will destroy you.'

— Jesus of Nazareth

TURNING POINT - BERTRAM

*A*ll my life I had wanted to be an actor, but it remained only a dream until something happened to remind me that it is not wise to sit on your dreams just because they seem wild or too difficult to achieve. I was at a conference in North Wales where the main message that came over to me was that it is so important to believe in yourself. I heard someone say 'the time to realise your dreams is **now'** and the words ricocheted me into hyperspace. An incredible thought came into my mind - 'start your own theatre group!'

It was a wonderful, exciting thought gushing through my awareness and thrilling me inside. Dare I? After the conference was over, I went home and pushed it to the back of my mind filed under 'improbable'; but my dream was not to be put aside so easily. A friend came to visit and casually mentioned that she had always wanted to put on a play. Before long we were talking excitedly about sharing our own theatre group. We were both seventeen and decided that the group should consist entirely of young people, so that we could prove to ourselves (and others) that we really could do it alone – even raising the money and sponsorship we were going to need.

Now my dream was on fire and nothing could stop it from blazing its glorious trail.

We wrote a basic story line for the first play and then looked round for people to fill the parts. After a few weeks we had an entire cast, a manager, a director, a composer (it was a musical) and I was the scriptwriter. The plot was based round the simple idea of seven young people who had shut themselves in a room until they could answer the question – Who are you? It gave us the chance to explore many beautiful issues (as well as problems) that arise from the process of self-examination.

From the time we had established our group it seemed as though God himself was supporting our production because the director of the theatre in Den-Bosch (where I live in the Netherlands) was so enthusiastic about our project that he allowed us to use the theatre rent-free. He even allowed us to use it during the fortnight before the performance so we could prepare our set. He got up early every Sunday morning, his only day off, to open the building so we could rehearse there and all he asked us to pay was 50% of our profit from the door money. What's more, my drama teacher offered us free use of a studio in the School of Performing Arts every weekend and we were also offered money for our production by the neighbouring town of Maastricht. Wow!

I can understand why a lot of young people don't make it when they try to fulfil their dream because the road can be very bumpy. Sometimes there is so much to do that I feel as if my head is going to explode, but I keep on walking straight towards my goal without looking back. Sometimes one of us falls, but we are all in it together, so we simply pick each other up and continue to walk on because we have a group dream. That dream is to be in the theatre, not in ten years' time, but *right now.* And we are realising our dream because we are putting our heart and soul into it. When people ask me how we have managed it, I say, 'Simple. With devotion, friendship, 1,000% motivation and with love.'

'Genius is 1% inspiration and 99% perspiration.'

Thomas Edison

I often wonder how it is possible for human beings to live their entire lives in ignorance of the extraordinary resources they have inside them. And so many people do live and die without ever tapping into their real potential. The problem is that people wait for the perfect time and conditions when they will be able to fire up on all cylinders and give the very best of themselves. It is such a strange attitude that insists we preserve our greatest wealth, keeping it tucked safely away in an inner vault like an investment to use some time in the future. Instead of going for it right now, in this living moment where the power lies, we are cautious and tentative about what may or may not happen. We delay while we ask ourselves when, where or why we should do something. Should we do it or shouldn't we?

All this just paralyses us and prevents us from giving 100% of ourselves to any situation.

The choice not to limit yourself in this way can create a major turning point in your life that offers incredible possibilities. Once you start to recognise and utilise the vast reservoir of natural resources within you, you will find it brings a tremendous sense of fulfilment into your life. It makes you more able to access the outer resources that are available to you. By 'outer resources' I mean anything that is external to you. It could be your family, your work, your money or your possessions.

Are you one of those people who say, 'One day I will...' or 'I'm waiting for things to change first?' Perhaps you are waiting to become healthier, older, richer or for your neighbour's cat to have kittens! This waiting is dangerous. It can make you feel lonely, unloved, under-used and useless, abused by a world that has it in for you.

Please don't wait for special moments or special people to come along. Remember - life is not a rehearsal. You may be waiting for a catalyst, but you are the catalyst. The turning point comes in discovering the inner resources, getting in tune and engaging with them. It's like discovering your keys on a piano or the strings on a guitar and deciding to tune them up to sound really great.

When Gandhi picked up a handful of salt on Dandi Beach it symbolised setting free a potential and soul force that was to change the course of history. Gandhi would probably say that you cannot afford to wait until you are as old as he was and to have lost all your teeth or parted with all your possessions before you pick up the handful of salt that liberates your potential and changes the course of your life forever.

Using your inner resources means tapping into your own potential, power, confidence and belief in yourself through tools such as meditation, relaxation, introspection and yoga. This will enable you to recognise and utilise inner resources that bring a sense of unity into your life. Then you are more capable of addressing the outer resources.

Outer resources can be channelled in such a way that they can make a difference to the world and to how you feel about your place in the universe. The game is much bigger than we originally thought. If you think you are only here for your personal agenda and that you don't really have anything to do with the world in general – think again.

Q Are you happy to give only 2% of your potential to this moment?

Q What decisions are you not responding to because you are waiting for something to change?

Q What is it that is stopping you from giving the highest of what you are at this moment?

TURNING POINT - BERTRAM

Q How balanced are your inner and outer worlds? Do you spend enough time exploring your inner resources? Or too much time dashing about in the world?

Turning

Point techniques

- Keep your inner thoughts high and noble and then relax in such a way that they start to come out and blend into your outer reality.

- Go from thoughts into action:
  Write down four things that will help you to engage. Simply by writing you have already begun.

- Each day at the same time do something that will bring you nearer to your goal or dream.

- Have an 'imagination' break each day. See all your dreams as accomplished and fulfilled and then watch the outer world blossom as a result. If you can imagine it - you can create it.

Your notes

Re-arrange
your values

'We do not see things as they are. We
see them as we are.'

The Talmud

TURNING POINT - JEAN

*E*verything was perfect. My son and daughter-in-law were taking me on an outing. We were enjoying the journey, glad of the opportunity to spend precious time together.

Without warning, the bus in front of us braked suddenly and we drove straight into the back of it. I had been sitting in the passenger seat and received serious injuries to my head and face. Some of my front teeth were broken and had to be replaced but my main struggle was in coming to terms with all the scars that disfigured my face. This was to haunt me for years. I had always been proud of my looks and spent hours in front of the mirror doing my make-up before I went out anywhere. I even insisted on looking glamorous in the office! Suddenly I couldn't go out anywhere because I couldn't risk letting anyone see my face. Using public transport was out of the question and consequently I hardly ever left the house.

It took me three years to find the courage to go back to work. During that time I forced myself to go by bus to visit my daughter. It made me physically sick. The next time I took the train. There was flooding on the line and we had to wait nearly two hours in the middle of the journey. Sitting on that train I had to face people. There was nowhere to hide. It didn't seem like it at the time, but that was the best thing that could have happened to me because it gave me the courage to start to go out a little more.

My return to work marked the beginning of a period of crisis for me. Three members of my close family were diagnosed as having cancer. It all came at once and my over-riding thought when I woke up every morning was 'Will I be next?' I seemed to be surrounded by fear. I tried to look after all the family and be everything to everyone – wife, mother, grandmother, sister, daughter and aunt. Before long I was physically burned out and, to add to the emotional insecurity I was still harbouring about the scars, I now found I had to contend with M.E., a severe chronic fatigue syndrome.

For a long time I struggled in the dark, not knowing which way to turn. Then two things happened to open up a new world to me. The first turning point was a gift from my husband. He had a small amount of money saved and gave it to me to buy something for myself. I bought a bike. Whenever I found the strength and energy, I would go out for a bike ride and the exercise gradually helped to oxygenate my system. This gave my energy levels an enormous boost.

The next thing that happened was that I was invited to a Dru Yoga seminar. It took a lot of courage for me to accept but once I got there all my doubts and fears fell away. My memories of that seminar have nothing to do with the physical yoga movements but of the all-embracing love I experienced there. For the first time in my life I had spent a day with people who seemed to have no other agenda than to accept and love the people they were with. I came away knowing that there was nothing wrong with me. The scars weren't important. There was no need to try to be this glamourous person I'd set myself up to be. I was fine just being me. It was a mind-blowing revelation.

Immediately I started going to a local Dru Yoga class and learned a few specific breathing and movement techniques that were to be the foundation of my physical and psychological recovery. It took some time and determination to come out of the M.E. but with regular practice of these techniques I managed to bounce back.

I had also begun to discover a vast reservoir of inner strength and joy, which were to support both me and my sister when she was diagnosed as having terminal cancer. For the final six months of her life I visited her regularly and my new-found joy gave us both the strength to face things together. On the day of her death the priest and doctors were at the house. They were all moved by the atmosphere of peace and love surrounding her. When the priest told me he could feel the love in the room I knew then that she had completed her journey happily and was all right wherever she was.

Today I look back on all the amazingly precious lessons that came out of that time. It was a steep but superb learning curve and I came through it all brilliantly with the help of my family and friends. I can now be strong for others and find that when people try to knock me it doesn't matter. I can deal with it thanks to the inner strength I have discovered. My life is now dedicated to helping other people through their own pain. I couldn't do that without being centred in myself and that is the gift my yoga practice has given me.

And my scars? Well, I have learned to love them. They have taught me so much I couldn't have learned otherwise and they have made me into the person I am today. Isn't that wonderful?

'You are not the clothes you have worn. You are not the jewellery you have bought. All that you are is a result of what you have thought.'

Eknath Easwaran

We all have different values based upon what we believe will lead us towards happiness and contentment. If you believe that people will only love you if you are rich, money will be your most important value. If your self-worth is attached to the way you look, your face and figure may be top of the list of priorities. Or perhaps it is how many presents you are able to give your kids at Christmas and birthdays that makes you feel good about yourself.

If your looks change will your happiness go too? And if you cannot compete with the gifts your neighbours are giving their children, will you become miserable?

Jean's story is a wonderful example of how life constantly challenges us to re-evaluate our priorities. Deciding to make health one of her major priorities was a real turning point for her. Once you decide to put energy into pleasing yourself and your body it can open up a whole new world for you and as Jean said, 'you discover a vast reservoir of inner strength and joy'.

Health is a good goal to strive for because it means you will eat well and exercise regularly. This also means you will feel better, live longer, be happier and make better decisions for your family. If health is your priority, you will be a better parent and/or boss because you feel better and calmer and will therefore have a clearer discrimination to be able to really help people. You won't need to buy things to make people happy because what you are will make them happy.

If your self-evaluation is based on superficial things, it is possible that you may need to re-assess your priorities and make some major adjustments.

Q What are your values based on? Do they make you happy or stressed? How do they affect others?

Q Where could you make changes that will benefit everyone in your life, including yourself?

Q What do you think makes you the person you are?

Turning

Point techniques

♦ Write down three things you want at the moment. What is the underlying value you hope to gain?

For instance, if you want a new car do you crave freedom?
Or to be seen as being successful?

If you want a relationship are you seeking security, excitement or comfort?
Or is it because you want to embark on a shared journey of discovery of how to love and be loved?

♦ Think of the three greatest moments of happiness you have ever experienced.
You might find they occurred because of your openness to life's beauty, rather than because of how much you owned, controlled or achieved. Perhaps your happiness is closer to you than you thought!

- Now list three things you could do today that would bring greater happiness, for example sending a card to all your friends to tell them how much they mean to you.

Your notes

Simplify
your life

'As you simplify your life, the laws of
the universe will be simpler; solitude will
not be solitude, poverty will not be poverty
nor weakness weakness.'

Henry David Thoreau

TURNING POINT - SALLY

*I*t was mid August in Biloxi, Mississippi, and the weather forecast was frightening. Hurricane Camille had taken a turn and was expected to hit the Gulf Coast within the next twenty-four hours. Living on a peninsula surrounded on three sides by water, the chances of serious flooding were very high. Being young and adventurous we toyed with the idea of staying to brave the storm. We decided not to because of the baby, as it was likely we could be days without water and electricity.

As we bundled all our necessities into the car the wind and rain had already started blowing hard. It was evening as we drove north and cars were lined up bumper to bumper at gas stations for blocks. As they ran out of gas they closed up and evacuated. We drove a hundred miles until we found a school which had opened as an emergency shelter. The wind howled louder and louder throughout the night and we lay awake listening.

Driving back the next morning we witnessed the first indications of damage. Telephone poles had snapped in half and dead cattle were lying in the fields. At that time we had no concept of the tangled devastation along the coast. As we approached what had been our neighbourhood, my husband Steve said it looked as if the entire area had been a Vietnam war zone. We had to walk the last half mile or so. There were other people about and we shared the silence of overwhelming shock. Not one house remained.

Everything was flattened except the thin sentinel pine trees, their bark peeled away at the ten foot mark above ground, the height to which the water had risen as the waves crashed across the narrow strip of land.

The place where our house had been was barely recognisable. A slab of cement with pipes from the kitchen and bathroom was sticking up and broken and everything else gone. And then we saw the angel. She was sitting upright facing us on the corner of the slab near the carport. She looked so beautiful sitting there serenely amidst the bleakness of devastation. A symbol of purity - and hope. I had stored our Christmas decorations on a shelf in the carport the January before Hurricane Camille. The angel had been wrapped in newspaper, stored in a box and placed on the shelf in the carport. The carport, boxes and paper were all gone. All around was broken devastation, whipped by wind and water. I picked up the angel which was made of ceramic. Her body had not one chip on it and not even the very delicate fingers of her hand were even slightly damaged. I stared at her in disbelief for a long time. She was trying to tell me something - that there was more to this hurricane than I was aware of at that moment.

Hurricane Camille was a big wake up call and the biggest lesson was that there are more important things in life than just 'things'. Having lost all my treasures, including the irreplaceable pictures of my youth, I realized how much I had been coveting these things. Suddenly I could see that I just didn't need them at all and this eventually brought a great feeling of freedom into my life that I had never felt before.

In the weeks that followed, my husband and I grew very, very close, communicating on a level we had never touched before. We had each realised how important we were to one another. The only thing that really mattered in life was that we had each other and our baby. We learned how much people matter too, because the crisis brought everyone in our neighbourhood together in the most incredible way. We all became gentle, open hearted people eager to help each other through our shared difficulties. We had time to give and to share, pooling food and sharing cook outs which tasted really wonderful no matter what was in them.

If your life is built on things that are fragile the forces of nature can take them away in a moment. My angel taught me that when you build your life on things that are solid and last forever, like love and friendship, they can never be taken away by any force on earth.

'There is no wealth but life.'

John Ruskin

We don't have to lose everything in one go like Sally did to realise what really matters in life. The feeling of freedom she described is available to us all once we can decide to let go our grasp on 'things'. And this letting go will make way for a new way of looking at what is really important in life and what is not. Gandhi always encouraged people to simplify their lives. He said that the simpler your life the better off you will be. The less you have, the less people will be able to manipulate you or make you do things you do not want to do. When Gandhi's followers, his *satyagrahis,* were imprisoned for civil disobedience General Smuts tried to get them to tow the line by ordering their soldiers to take away their possessions. They didn't have any. He suggested starving them into submission. They were already fasting. He couldn't find anything to take away from them because they had nothing.

The more simple your lifestyle and the fewer demands you have on other people, the less stressed you will be and the more you can give to others. You will also have more time for yourself, family and friends. One of the best ways to have a calm, confident mind is to simplify your needs.

Most of us are surrounded by things we never really use but are keeping 'just in case'. When you truly believe in the principle that you are always provided with everything you need, events in your life will prove it to be true. When Gandhi was asked to sum up the message of the great Indian scripture, the Bhagavad Gita, he said it in three words. 'Renounce and enjoy. This is the secret to happiness,' he said. Throughout history wise people in every culture have found it to be true that real happiness can never be found in wanting more and more.

Q Do you really need all the clutter in your life?

Q What would you do to simplify your life today? What can you do at home? At work?

Q What is the most solid thing in your life now?

Q Which of your possessions couldn't you bear to lose?

Turning

Point techniques

- Why not start clearing out your house?
  A good rule to follow is this: If you haven't used it for a year, you don't need it. If the prospect seems too daunting you could begin with one room, or even one drawer. As you let go of 'things' notice how much lighter you feel inside.

- Write as fast as you can without stopping for two minutes. Without thinking make a list of all the things that are really important to you. This process will help you review what is essential and non essential in your life. Try it!

Your notes

Look on the bright side

'We don't laugh because we're happy,
we're happy because we laugh.'

William James

*B*eing in the army means I often have to work in situations that are potentially quite physically and emotionally overwhelming. If you do not have a coping strategy that is.

A few years ago I was posted to Rwanda as part of a UN peace keeping force. We had gone out with two specific briefs. We took heavy duty digging equipment with us to dig mass graves for thousands of dead bodies. Then we were to repair and rebuild many of the roads that had been destroyed during the fighting. It was a mammoth task and we worked ourselves and the machinery very hard until the plant finally broke down. As it was not possible to get it repaired straight away we were faced with a choice. We could either sit around waiting for something to happen or we could make something happen. We chose the latter option and volunteered to help the medical teams who were not able to meet the demands placed on them. We were soon busy inoculating hundreds of people and cleaning up serious machete wounds. We were using gentian violet (a purple antiseptic tincture) to dress the wounds and someone had the bright idea of painting huge gentian violet coloured smiles on the children's faces as they queued up to be inoculated. The children loved it and were soon clamouring to be painted. The painted smiles quickly turned into real smiles and it felt like we had all been helped by the process.

It was sometimes gruelling work but the interesting thing is that none of my squadron had to undergo de-traumatisation when we returned home whereas many others did.

I've thought about this a lot and realise that how you survive emotionally in any situation depends not so much on the situation itself as on the way you look at things. Some people had no problems during the waiting period when our machinery broke down. They were the ones who kept happiest and even spent time larking around like kids. It sounds silly but they were the ones who were less aggressive with each other and suffered the least afterwards.

The ones who were most upset about being out of their normal environment and routine were the ones who lost their tempers most often. Our training had prepared us to go out to meet any situation at any time. Now we were in 'the situation' we had to use that energy or it somehow turned in on us. It was a case of 'managing our adrenaline'. When we were working with the medical team we all made a point of laughing and joking with the patients and their families - sometimes in quite an outrageous way.

Some people criticised us for our cheerfulness, accusing us of being unfeeling and even callous, as though responding with misery is an indication that you care. But I'm convinced that this is what enabled us to maintain our sanity and emotional balance - and do a good job at the same time. Allowing yourself to be weighed down by the situation you are in doesn't help anyone and only serves to make you ineffective at what you have to do. I would advise anyone to try to remain cheerful and active no matter what is happening around them or to them and they will discover, as I did, that it really works.

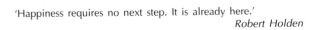

'Happiness requires no next step. It is already here.'
Robert Holden

We all know what it feels like to be with someone who is happy. It makes us happy too, and because we are happy it affects everyone we are with, starting a chain reaction that can lead to an explosion of happiness. The opposite is also true but who wants to be responsible for starting a chain reaction that leads to an explosion of sadness and pain?

If we are not careful we can make life much too serious and become unaware that we have imprisoned our minds into a cage that doesn't know how to celebrate life any more. We may go out once a month to 'enjoy ourselves' for a meal or a film, but why don't we make every meal a celebration?

Happiness is a state of mind. Can you imagine always feeling the way you did the day you passed your driving test? Or graduated? That feeling of elation comes from your deep inner soul - and it doesn't have to be locked away and only released on special occasions. It really is possible to feel that way all the time if you just give yourself permission to.

Imagine waking up every morning and saying, 'Let's celebrate today!' Gandhi did it at almost every junction in his life. In fact one thing you could say about Gandhi is that no matter what difficulties came his way he always met them with a great sense of humour and joy. Even when the police came to arrest him after the Salt March he was ready to go with a smile on his face and on the way to the prison he chatted with his captors as if they were old friends.

Begin to discover methods, attitudes and approaches to daily life that give you enough good reasons to celebrate. And when we can learn to rejoice in the normal mundane things we can learn to celebrate when things get really tough.

Q   Can you smile in the face of difficulty?

Q   When did you last try to make someone laugh?

Q   What makes you laugh most?

Q   What can you celebrate today?

Turning Point techniques

Have you ever noticed that when you have had a really good laugh all agitated thinking stops? In fact, it is impossible to laugh and be upset.

- So every morning as you wake up, give yourself a good stretch. Close your eyes and put your hand on your upper abdomen. Breathe in and as you breathe out say HA! Say it again and again and again and soon you won't be able to stop yourself laughing. Do it for five minutes. It will change your whole day!

- Buy a book of humorous stories and practise telling them to someone.

- Do something outrageous that will make you feel like a child again. Play football with the kids in the street, have a pillow fight, have an un-birthday party - anything that will allow you to have fun and also 'manage your adrenaline'.

- Write down everything you have done today that has made you happy. Do it more often!

Your notes

Look for the best in people

When you meet your friend on the roadside or in the market place, let the spirit in you move your lips and direct your tongue. Let the voice within your voice speak to the ear of his ear for his soul will keep the truth of your heart as the taste of the wine is remembered when the colour is forgotten and the vessel is no more.

— Kahlil Gibran

TURNING POINT - DEREK

*I*t was a 'chance' conversation resulting from a 'chance' meeting but this one statement by one man changed my whole life. I realised for the first time just what a responsibility I have to think before I speak and to choose every word very, very carefully.

The man was telling me about his childhood in India. According to their custom, when a child reached a certain age a palmist would be called in to read their palm. On the appointed day the palmist arrived to examine him and the family stood by eagerly waiting to hear the outcome. Would their son become a famous scholar? A wealthy businessman? Or maybe a great doctor? None of them were prepared for what the palmist had to say: *'This child has no lifeline!'* he announced. *'Which means he will always be unlucky.'*

Although the boy was too young to understand the implications of this statement, his family certainly did and they began to relate to him according to this dire prediction. From that time on nobody really expected very much of him and he was consequently blamed for all the accidents and misfortunes that came upon the family. And this is the environment he grew up in.

That one sentence was to affect the image people had of him for many years to come. Even the boy himself believed that he would never make anything of his life. However, as he grew up there was a part of him that longed to be respected and successful.

He even cherished dreams of receiving a good education. Thinking that there was no point in paying out hard-earned money to pay for an education that would never come to anything his family refused to finance him. However, as time went on he became more and more determined and when he was sixteen he decided to find a way to pay for his own education.

He had to look for a job and accommodation. Neither was easy to find but eventually he came across one landlord who agreed to take him in if he promised to pay all his wages as rent.

He didn't even have a job at this stage and in desperation felt he had to be honest with his landlord from the outset. 'I'll do my very best,' he said, 'but I must tell you that I'm always unlucky.' And he explained the whole situation. The landlord looked interested and asked to see his palm. He studied it for a few moments and then looked keenly at the young man. 'Don't you realise what that means?' he asked. 'It means you are a very rare human being with total control over your destiny!'

The words struck the young man like lightning. He couldn't believe it! He was so excited by the possibility that those words contained that he couldn't even sleep and for the first time in his life he began to believe that he might be able to achieve something. As his thoughts changed he also began to think differently about himself. This made him act differently and it wasn't long before his fortune started to change as well. He went to university and soon afterwards moved to England where he ran a very successful business for many years.

Years later he returned to his village in India and when he saw his old landlord he ran up to him, bowed down and touched his feet in gratitude for the few words that had changed his fortune all those years ago. 'Ah,' said the landlord, 'you must be the lucky boy!'

'The shoe that fits one man pinches another.'

Carl Jung

Every morning my mother used to place a plate of dry leaves outside the door of our little house in Kenya and every day the wind would blow them away. When I asked her why she kept doing this she told me that it was to remind herself that just as the leaves can never be brought back once the wind had blown them away, so it is with our words. They can never be taken back no matter how hard we try to make amends.

Words that are critical or unkind in any way have the power to hurt, alienate and even destroy a person. I once knew a woman whose whole life had been destroyed by a 'chance remark' someone had made one day suggesting she was overweight. This had hurt her so much that she had stopped eating altogether. By the time I met her, her anorexia was so advanced that there was hardly anything left of her or her life.

Have you ever noticed that you always think that you are right? But everyone does! Now consider the implications. It is only too easy to find fault with others if the way they live or the things they do, do not match our beliefs. We may judge them as 'odd' or even 'wrong'. But I wonder if we ever stop to consider the effect this might have on the other person's life?

Whenever I feel inclined to pass judgement on someone or something they are doing I always remind myself that that person probably feels just as doubtful about some of the things I do in my life. It is not a question of being right or wrong. It is simply a question of doing things differently. There is a story in my tradition that tells of three men who were blindfolded and led to a forest where a small elephant was grazing. Each man was asked to feel what was in front of him and then to say what he thought it was. One held the trunk and thought it was a rope. One thought the tail was a snake, another was sure the thick, rough skinned leg was a tree. Each man was right in his own way. We each see life from the limited perspective of our own experience and talents and that is unique to each one of us.

Q Do you have a tendency to be critical?

Q Have you criticised someone today, either verbally or mentally? How did it feel?

Q How many kind and beautiful words have you used today towards yourself and others?

Q What could you do to support instead of judge?

Turning

Point techniques

- Whenever you feel the impulse to judge or criticise ask yourself three questions:
  Is what I am going to say kind?
  Is it truthful?
  Is it necessary?
  If the answer to any of these questions is 'no' think very, very carefully before speaking.

- Simply remember that people say one thing but often mean to convey something else. We then hear and distort it through our own perceptions. Listen deeply to the intention and the hidden meaning behind people's words and actions.

- Treat each person as if they were you. How would *you* like to be treated? Give love, simply because that is what you would want to receive. Try to become aware of who the source is inside that person, rather than the physical frame and personality. It will stop you judging.

Your notes

You can
do it!

'The way I change my life is to act as if
I am the person I really want to be.'

Ashley Montagu

*E*ven though I am very used to disabled students, when Bill was first wheeled into the classroom I couldn't really imagine how he was possibly going to be able to cope. He had been completely paralysed from birth due to a brain stem injury and the only way he could communicate was through blinking his eyes - open for 'yes' and closed for 'no' - which had to be interpreted by his full time helper. It was an arduous process for both of them. He had arrived late in the term and I was uneasy about his ability to catch up. Bill was so insistent that he would be able to do this, however, that I had to reluctantly agree to let him stay.

Bill turned out to have the best attendance in the class and was an extremely attentive student who listened carefully despite the spasmodic muscle contractions and tremors that went through his body from time to time. He also made gurgling sounds over which he obviously had no control and which appeared not to distract him from his concentration. I was very impressed by this young boy's determination to get a degree against these almost impossible odds.

The exam was a painful experience both for him and his helper - as well as for me to watch. His helper had to review each question and then to follow Bill's blinking eyes as to the correct multiple choice answer. It was a very tedious and time intensive process, slowed down even more by his periodic muscle spasms. In fact, it took him twice as long as any other student to complete the test. Many times I was tempted to suggest that he be exempted from the ordeal, but there was something about Bill that told me how important it was for him to finish. When I marked the papers I was so glad that I had not stopped him because to my amazement he scored the highest in the class with an A+! The look on his face when he found out was one of the most beautiful sights I have ever seen and one that I shall never be able to forget.

Bill is only twenty-one years old and despite his quadriplegia he has leadership abilities that extend beyond his studies to working on committees and campaigning for other disabled people. His aid told the class one day that he campaigns on behalf of other challenged people as well as being a full time student. I have no doubt that Bill is going to get his sociology degree. He has taught me one very important lesson - that there are no obstacles in life when you are determined to dream the impossible dream.

This song resonates with the hope of students who do not empower obstacles but rather believe in their abilities no matter what stands in their way. They are the ones who not only achieve their hopes and dreams, but inspire those of us with more advantages but less faith.

'Find something in life about which you can say, ''This is my joy.'' '

Bernie Siegel

When you hear about people like Bill who achieve incredible things that seem impossible to us, you can use it as an inspiration to face your own seemingly impossible difficulties. And when someone you admire accomplishes something very special, there are always two ways to take it. You can exclude yourself from their category, thinking there is something special about them - or you can choose to think, 'If they have done it, so can I!'

Say you were an aspiring flute player, for instance, and you went to see a flautist performing beautifully in concert. You could keep a distance between yourself and his skill or you could say, 'I'm going to be like that.' It's a simple paradigm but it actually puts you in a place where you can make a miracle happen.

Once you start doing this you begin to empower a life that can never be boring or pessimistic again. Just as geese fly in V formation so that each can take a turn to be at the head of the flock, you learn by seeing the others at the front. You recognise you have the same potential and ability although perhaps your flying style is different and you go at a different speed. The potential is there nonetheless.

Perhaps the greatest obstacle to success that anyone ever experiences is the emotional fear of what people will say if they fail. Success is built on top of many not-so-perfect attempts so you will need to become 'good at failing' in order to be successful. If you find the fear of failure is a problem for you, I recommend Mansukh's book 'Crisis and the Miracle of Love' which has a very useful chapter on overcoming the obstacles to success.

Q Do you believe that the world owes you something or that you owe the world something?

Q Do you believe that for anything to be worthwhile you have to perform perfectly or do you think that the journey is more important than the results?

Q What can you do today to help yourself to achieve the impossible?

Turning

Point techniques

- Every time you see amazing people and talents just say to yourself, 'I can do it too,' no matter how impossible it may appear to you.

- Every time you think you can't do something, remember Bill and ask yourself if your difficulties are any more insurmountable than his.

- Maybe your health won't allow you to achieve a lot of things on a physical level but you can make sure that you do achieve something within the limitations of your own capacities. If you only have half an hour in the day when you feel fit enough to do anything, make that half hour really count.

- Think of something small you have always wanted to do but have considered to be totally impossible. Do it.

- Think of something big you have always wanted to do. Write it down at the top of a piece of paper and look at it very closely for at least thirty seconds. Think of three things you could do *now* that will move you in the direction of your goal.

- For example, if you want to be a pop star - go out and buy a guitar! Or record a song on your portable tape recorder. If you want to fly a plane go and meet a pilot - at least it's a start!

Your notes

Take time to watch the sunrise

'In the hope of reaching the moon, men fail to see the flowers that blossom at their feet.'

Albert Schweitzer

TURNING POINT - CORIEN

I had always lived an active life until about five years ago when I started to develop a lot of back pain. I knew I should rest but I had so many things to do .... I worked part-time as a nurse and was also attending acting classes. The acting was a real passion with me. But ignoring the back problem didn't make it go away, of course, and I eventually had to agree to have an operation. Soon I was feeling wonderful again and back at work and my acting class. Life was very busy. 'Ho, ho!' said my back.... Another operation.... And it wasn't long before I felt wonderful again and I was soon back at work and acting with a theatre group. I got some good parts to play and life was exciting. I sometimes thought that I should be spending more time with my husband and four young children but I had to make a choice..... and my husband was very kind. He just wanted me to enjoy my life. Then my back started to hurt again. I couldn't believe it and tried to pay no attention to it, until I woke up one morning unable to move my leg or empty my bladder.

Hospital tests revealed lots of problems with my back but the only solution offered was bed rest and pain-killers. In hospital I shared a room with an old lady who was very ill. When she was well enough she would talk to me about her life and we would laugh and joke together. One day she was moved to another part of the hospital. She cried and hugged me as she told me how much she would miss me. That really made me think. What was I? Who was I?

Why was this happening to me? Although my body didn't work as it should, I could still mean something to someone. I could still make jokes. I could still be .... me...... So I was not this body. I was much, much more. I was my mind and my spirit. What exactly was it that made up the complete me? And what was the purpose of my life? There were so many questions. I even began to think about God. I had always laughed at the idea, but somehow I wasn't so sure any more. All this trouble with my back.... it was like 'someone' was trying to tell me something. What was 'it' trying to say? Perhaps it was time I began to listen. Better late then never.

I shared all these feelings and questions with a friend who came to visit me regularly while I was in hospital for all those weeks. She understood and brought me books to read that helped me understand more about spirituality. One day she brought me the Bhagavad Gita, a beautiful book from the Indian tradition that explains very clearly the exact nature of man. The story begins when Arjuna, a warrior famous for his great skill and courage, is about to start battle. Arjuna is standing between the two armies with his friend and teacher, Krishna, and recognises that his main opponents are his closest relatives and dearest friends. He knows that he is being asked to fight a righteous war but shrinks from the prospect of having to kill his own family. The situation forces him to face his own fears and accept the challenge of letting go of everything that has been familiar and comforting to him. It is only when Krishna explains the true nature of man and his relationship with himself, with life and with God that he is able to gather together his courage and enter the battle. I didn't really understand what it meant and couldn't take in the part when Krishna told Arjuna that each one of us has our own particular role and responsibility in life and we neglect it at our peril. My mind was busy with other things because they were thinking of transferring me to another hospital a long way from home.

Soon after arriving at the new hospital the surgeon told me that there was a possibility they could help me but it would mean a very long and difficult operation with no guarantee of success. If I did decide to have the operation I would have to spend three months lying in bed in plaster afterwards. I was frightened and didn't know what to do. I wanted to read a book to take my mind off things but the only one I could find was this 'Gita'. I began to read it again and suddenly I realised that I was Arjuna! The operation was my battle. I suddenly knew that I had to do it. I had to fight my battle and Krishna would be there to help me. There was no need to worry. God really was there.

The night after the operation I had the most beautiful experience. I awoke to a lot of commotion round my bed as doctors and nurses rushed to tend to me. I knew I was very ill and thought I was going to die but, at the same time, I felt very calm, surrounded by a peaceful, tender atmosphere and a beautiful bright light. My husband and children were there. It was so beautiful that I can't find words to describe it adequately. Then I felt needles in my leg and the light was gone. I must have slept then because the next thing I remember was waking up in the morning knowing I would get better. And the most important thing I had to do was to take care of my husband and the children. They needed me.

Then followed three months of lying in bed in plaster. During that time I read and re-read the Gita as well as watching videos about it on television. Each time I read it I understood it better and realised that it offered a very beautiful and practical model for living my life. After three months the plaster was removed. Now, six months later, I'm still receiving therapy but my body functions normally again and I don't have any more pain. I feel great and have never been so happy before. I often feel like singing all day. Sometimes I do! The doctor says it's a miracle. I know it's God.

'As you walk and eat and travel, be where you are, otherwise you will miss most of your life.'

Jack Kornfield

Are you one of those people who get up in the morning and rush into the day, hardly noticing the people around you? Do you find that you are so intent to get everything done that needs to be done that your days go by in a frenzy of activity? Does your day rush past so quickly you hardly seem to have time to get up before it's time to go back to bed? Somehow there always seems to be so much to do and so little time to do it!

When we are busy all the time - even busy with good things - the frenzy of activity neutralises our capacity to feel peaceful inside. Frantic rushing creates unnecessary suffering for us as well as others around us, but our whole culture it seems, has become based on busyness. Perhaps that is why so many people are unhappy. It's worth remembering that nobody on their death bed ever wished they had worked harder...

Not only can we miss the glory of each sunrise, we also miss the whole of the sun's journey across the sky, not to mention the sunset at the end of the day, simply because we are *too busy*. Without quality time we lack real gratitude. This also goes for all the wonders in our life - including the friends, children and events that we all take for granted. Do you remember when you were a child and every day stretched out endlessly before you? And the summer holidays seemed to last forever? How about now?

Please take time to appreciate your life - the sunrise, the stars, your relationships - with children, friends, workmates and partners and all the other things that enrich your life beyond measure. If you can 'clunk-click' into gratitude every morning it will make it almost impossible to do yourself or anyone else any kind of injury. If you wake up to gratitude you can only have a good day!

Q How often do you tell others how much they mean to you?

Q When was the last time you watched the sunrise?

Q When did you last play frisbee or tag? How much did you enjoy it?

Turning

Point techniques

- If you feel you do not have enough time to do something, find someone who appears to be fitting a lot into their day and ask them how they do it. You both have the same number of hours in a day.

- Don't waste time thinking and worrying about how much you have to do. Tell yourself you have got time, and you will have.

- When you want to do something, make sure you really want to do it and that you are not just responding to subtle pressure from the media or friends. There will be enough time in your life to do whatever you need to do.

- Go out into nature and stand among the trees. Look at the sky. Look at the earth. And just for a moment consider all the things you have ever done. Ask yourself, 'What do these really matter now? How is it now?'

- Five Seconds Strategy for ending 'busyness': Stop! Clap your hands and then look at your palms and smile. Either you will feel so silly you will have to laugh at yourself for getting caught up in busyness again...or your heart will open and you will experience an unexpected feeling of happiness. Try it! And slow down!

- Draw three reasons why you should be busy today. Do you really want to live in the world you have just drawn?

- What you do first thing in the morning will set the energy for the rest of the day. As you wake up, take time to be with yourself, and be aware of how you are breathing.
  Affirm: 'I have the time and space to accomplish all that needs to be done.'

Your notes

Speak your truth

'When one man speaks his truth the whole world wins...'

Gandhi

TURNING POINT - MOON

*O*urs was an unconventional marriage as, coming from an Islamic-Bengali background, I had been expected and encouraged to marry someone of my own race and religion. My chosen husband, Jim was an Englishman whom I met whilst studying for my first degree. I was attracted to the deep insights he shared about various spiritual disciplines and philosophies and I admired and respected him for this. In him I had found a true partner with whom I could share my own spiritual quest.

Our first months of marriage were exciting - learning to live and share responsibilities together in a tiny South London flat. I came to know his habits and ways of thinking and did my best to change according to the needs of the relationship. I also grew to love his family and especially his mother who was supportive and happy about our marriage.

Two years into the marriage Jim embarked on the process of self-discovery. This was a new and rather bewildering world for me. As he began to explore his emotions and how they affected his relationships on a deep level I began to feel excluded from his life. I just didn't understand what was going on. Over the years his search took him down many different avenues and it seemed to me that I was being left further and further behind. He couldn't communicate what he was discovering in a way that meant something to me and I was totally unable to ask the right questions. This inability to communicate spilled over into the rest of our lives and a wall of silence developed between us. I felt totally lost. I desperately wanted to make the marriage work but had no idea how to bridge the chasm that was opening up between us.

One day I discovered an old postcard in my drawer. It was an unusual picture of an Indian deity. It reminded me somehow of the need for prayer, and I put it on my bedside table and lit a candle. It was the first time I had ever really prayed and it became the turning point in my search for a solution to the situation. During my times of prayer I began to receive subtle messages. I was bewildered at first, but as they were always full of hope and positivity I began to listen and to trust them more closely.

One message was, 'Re-define yourself!' and from that I realised I needed to change my image of myself. Rather than seeing myself as being helpless I needed to look at myself as a powerful person. Another strong message said, 'I am calling you.' I could feel this message physically in my body as a pulse and I knew it was coming from my soul. Through prayer I was beginning to discover an invincible and indestructible part of myself. Things began to change.

I felt new horizons opening up to me. I knew there were aspects of my life to be explored that I had been totally unaware of before. This must have been the position Jim had found himself in years before when he had started to investigate new areas of personal growth. It's a wonderful situation to be in – slightly scary but very, very exciting – and I didn't want to let it go. I began to understand that my silence had been due to a fear of being rejected. Now I was stronger in myself I was learning to value my own needs and to respect his feelings in a way I hadn't been able to before. I also became happier and happier with my life. Challenges didn't get me down in the way they had done before and my whole world started to look different. I discovered a joyful lightness inside me and even found myself singing in the shower again! Even when it became clear to both of us that our paths lay in different directions the separation didn't break me as I had once feared it would. I had found myself and was excited at the next phase of my life which was opening up in front of me.

'I never get angry, I just grow tumours.'

Woody Allen

Are you one of those people who never say what they are really feeling, bottling things up inside instead so as not to 'cause trouble'? Perhaps you are afraid that if you speak your mind people will not like you, will reject you or, even worse, leave? But somewhere deep inside you there must be a longing to be able to break free and to be honest and true to yourself and others.

I don't know if you have ever seen the film 'Liar Liar', in which the actor Jim Carey portrayed a man who seemed completely unable to tell the truth. He was always saying one thing and doing another. When he didn't turn up for his son's birthday - after promising he would be there - his son made a heartfelt wish as he blew out his candles that his father would tell the truth *just for one day.* Such was the little boy's longing that it actually happened and his father found himself saying things that were completely true all day. Of course it created havoc in his business life and relationships because he was suddenly having to be honest, but it also transformed his life - and him.

There is a great power in truth and if we bottle up or deny our own truth to be socially acceptable, we are actually living a lie.

This can create blocks inside us that may turn into mini time bombs. Untruth creates disunity. If, for example, you bought a car for £200 and then offered it for sale for £450, telling the potential buyer it cost you £300 how would that affect you? Although you moved into the situation as one person, you will move out of it as *three.* Now your intellect knows the truth, your mind bargains with the truth and your mouth distorts the truth, you will have become fragmented, splitting your mind in three ways. The consequence will be that when you next set yourself a task to do, you will quite simply not be able to achieve it.

It takes courage and love to tell the truth because perhaps people will not always like what you say - but they will always respect you for it, even if they do not admit it. What is more important however, is that you will respect yourself. It does not feel good to hold back from what you know is right and when you find the courage to speak out it releases a tremendous power and energy inside you. It feels really good, if a little scary at first.

I recently heard about a young man who loved playing the violin and longed to be a professional violinist. His parents, however, wanted him to become a lawyer, which is what he did. Still in his early twenties, he developed a brain tumour and was given only one year to live. He decided to give up his job and spend the whole of that year playing his violin. A year later he was playing in a concert orchestra - without a brain tumour. It had completely gone.

Please don't wait until you only have a year to live to tell the truth about what you really want and feel! There are times when we have to stand up for what is right and not be a witness to negativity. If you tune into your deeper, inner self, your intuition will tell you what to say and who to say it to.

Allow the true you to emerge untainted by what other people may think of you and feel the freedom and joy of just being yourself.

Q How often do you seethe in silence when you know you should speak up?

Q What are you going to do the next time you feel 'put down'?

Q Do you think it is selfish to voice your own thoughts and needs?

Q Are you the person you want to be?

Q In what ways do you tend to live your life for others?

♦ We are often trained in the west to give to others, but we forget that giving means 50% honouring the people around us and 50% respecting the greatness we have within ourselves. Make sure you spend *as much energy as you give to others* to developing your own inner wellbeing.

♦ Even St. Francis, perhaps the greatest giver in the western world since Jesus, used to rush back into the mountains as soon as he felt his light beginning to wane. In fact he would often drop a conversation in mid-sentence! If it was OK for someone like him to spend time looking after his own needs, it's absolutely vital that we should.

♦ Sit in silence.

♦ Affirm a thought that honours you, for example: 'I am now able to speak my truth.'

- Carry yourself as if you were the greatest person you know.

- Practise every day telling your truth even once. Be very aware when you are holding back.

- Remember that at the deepest level you cannot be hurt. If you cannot speak your truth then make sure you live it.

Your notes

No Problem!

'For a long time it seemed to me that life was about to begin - real life. But there was always some obstacle in the way, something to be got through first, some unfinished business, time still to be served, a debt to be paid. Then life would begin. At last it dawned on me that those obstacles were my life.'

— Fr. Alfred D' Souza

*I*t is no secret that the teenage years can be very turbulent ones and I think it is true to say that I experienced all the drama and excitement in full techni-colour. Having been passed from one foster home to another until I was adopted at the age of four, my childhood had been very disrupted and all my insecurity came to the surface in my teens. Afraid to totally give or receive love through fear that I might be rejected, I nevertheless took every opportunity to seek attention and love. I gave my parents a really hard time and finished up getting pregnant when I was sixteen. This was a traumatic time for me because, before I had realised that I was pregnant, my partner had returned to Trinidad to visit his family for six months. For three months I didn't hear from him and was unable to contact him. Would he really come back to support me? Coping with the pregnancy in these circumstances was difficult enough but I was still at school studying for my exams at the same time. I was worn out, frightened and desperately lonely.

There was no way I could have known at the time, but this pregnancy was to be the making of me. All I knew then was that I wasn't coping and didn't know where to turn for help. One night as I lay in bed I was in such a state of panic, I found myself calling out to someone – anyone – who might be there to come and help me. Exhausted, I finally fell asleep.

In the middle of the night I woke up. In front of me was a

beautiful bright light of a kind I had never seen before. The whole room was filled with brightness and light and warmth and love. These are the best words I can find to describe the experience, although they do not do justice to what I was feeling. I was also aware of a presence behind me. I can only say that I knew there was an angel there, holding me tight and telling me, 'It's going to be all right. Everything's going to be all right.' I had always been afraid of 'things happening in the dark' but there was something that was totally reassuring and comforting about this experience. It was to change my life, although its effects only made themselves apparent gradually over the coming months and years.

When my son was born it felt as though I had met my soul mate. He was – and still is - the light of my life. When he was small I started to expand my horizons and read books that introduced me to the world of spirituality. I read about guardian angels, auras and the powerful effect that the mind has on our overall state of well-being. I was beginning to realise that there was a lot more to life than I had discovered so far and that this is what I had been searching for in the wrong places during my turbulent teenage years. My search now took a new turn and my journey took me away from the barren territory of fear, insecurity and inner turmoil into a welcoming land of trust, self-confidence, happiness and inner peace. My life was beginning to take off.

TURNING POINT - NATASHA

My adoptive parents are the kindest and most caring people you could ever hope to meet, yet I had never been able to allow myself to love them completely. The fear of being rejected again had always held me back. Now that I was a mother myself and was gaining an insight into the nature of the love that exists between parents and their children, I was able to let go of my fears and love them without reservation. Now I am closer to them than I ever was before.

When my son was three my father was elected Lord Mayor and he asked me to be the mayoress. One day he was invited to my old school to make the presentations on prize-giving day. My reputation as a difficult student had obviously lived on after I had left because I was requested not to join my father on the occasion. However, he sent back an ultimatum – if I couldn't go, he wouldn't go either. When we arrived at the school I was overwhelmed by the kind reception I received from the teachers there. They were genuinely happy to see that I had made something of my life and it was evident to me that I had reached an important new landmark in my own growth.

Now I have a job as part-time youth worker, helping youngsters from areas reputed to be the most difficult in the borough. I also work in a nursing home, caring for patients who are terminally ill with Parkinson's disease. If I had been told six years ago that I would be doing this I would just have laughed but, again, I have gained so much from the experience. I have learned to see beyond the body and its physical limitations to find the human being within. I know that everyone has bodily challenges from time to time and also that anyone might go off the rails at some time in their life. But that isn't what matters. People need loving and nurturing and, if you give them what they need, they will always return it to you many times over.

I have also gained the confidence and commitment to speak up for other people's rights even in the face of authority. I am a school governor, have appeared on a T.V. talk show about teenage parents and have been involved in producing sex education videos. I am twenty two now. I have my own family with two beautiful children and I am happy. I don't dwell on the past. I just get on with my life and enjoy it.

'Some of the most exciting opportunities come cleverly disguised as impossible difficulties.'

Bernie Siegel

My own life has always been full of challenge and difficulty and I really wouldn't have it any other way. From a very early age my mother always encouraged me to meet difficulties with the same grace as a gazelle that delicately leaps over obstacles without touching them. From the very earliest days she and my father were keen to instil a clear certainty that it is the most difficult things in life that contain the most priceless gifts.

Every day people come to me with an endless stream of problems to sort out. So many in fact, that if I had not developed this kind of positive attitude it would be very easy to feel overwhelmed and depressed instead of excited and challenged by them.

It always brings a smile to my face when I think of the story of the man who was bitterly complaining to his friend one day about the fact that his life was constantly plagued by problems. He just couldn't come to terms with the fact that no sooner had he resolved one than four or five others would replace it. He was at his wits end as to know what to do. His friend offered to take him to a place he knew of where there were at least 25,000 people who didn't have any problems or even a care in the world. 'Take me there!' said the man. 'I want to talk to them!' His friend laughed and explained, 'It's our local cemetery!'

Problems are part of life and I believe that they are presented to us purposefully because we need to discover the greatness we have within ourselves and not to stay small and limited. It is the very difficulties and problems we face every single day that push us beyond the limitations and confines of our comfort zone. They force us to draw on resources we don't even know we have and in so doing discover much greater levels of inspiration and creativity within ourselves. I always like to remember the immortal words of Gandhi when he said, 'I have not the shadow of a doubt that any man or woman can achieve what I have, if he or she would make the same effort and cultivate the same hope and faith.'

Q Do you approach obstacles in life with courage, tenacity and humour? Or do you allow yourself to become overwhelmed by them?

Q Do you discuss your problems at length with people in an attempt to resolve them? Does it work?

Q How much time are you spending focusing on the problem? And the solution?

Q Do you keep your problems pent up inside so they burn you up? How do you open to their rewards?

Turning

Point techniques

- Whenever you go through a bad patch try to remember that there are always many things you can do to change either the situation or the way you are looking at it.

- If you find yourself turning to the bottle or a chocolate bar to avoid unpleasantness - stop! Think again! If you can allow yourself to enter fully into the experience of each moment you will have no regrets at the end of the day.

- What appears immediately as a big mistake, looked upon in the long term may have many profitable outcomes. The single most important factor is to develop an inner strength that will enable you to be untouched by the situation. Sit in silence every day to help you to gain inner strength.*

* See Face to Face with Life for useful meditation techniques

Turning

Point

- Read stories about famous people like Abraham Lincoln who have managed to overcome impossible odds. He failed at almost everything he did but eventually became President because he refused to give up and never accepted failure.

- Give 10% of your energy to the problem and 90% to the solutions.

- Give yourself a provisional time limit. Say to yourself 'I will solve this by.... I need an answer by...'

- When confronted by a problem, immediately think of a solution and implement it straight away. Yes! Pick up that phone now....

Problems faced and dealt with **now** are called opportunities. Problems left till **later** are called crises. You have all the resources you need to deal with the challenges life gives you in the instant they come. But

if you leave it till later, all the energy available to turn
the challenge into opportunity will have evaporated.
You will be left with a *problem* on your hands.

Your notes

Use suffering wisely

'If we could see everything, even
tragedy, as a gift in disguise, we would
then find the best way to nourish the soul.'
Elizabeth Kubler-Ross

TURNING POINT - JOAN

*A*s I leaned down tenderly to pick up my two day old son Ben, I was still enveloped in the euphoria of mother love that surrounds a woman when she has just given birth to a new life. You can never explain to anyone else the rush of feeling that comes into your heart when you take that tiny form into your arms and cradle it to your breast. But my euphoria was short lived. His body, though warm, was limp and lifeless. I suddenly felt seized by fear. I couldn't see any movement of breath.....I quickly pulled a piece of thread from his blanket and held it under his nose. It didn't move.

Almost paralysed by fear and panic I ran towards the phone. I had to get help. The doctor seem to take forever in coming and all the time I held on to my little son, completely unable to believe that God was taking back this beautiful gift. I felt confused and ill-equipped to grasp the reality of the situation. It didn't take long after the doctor came to realise that he was not going to be able to resuscitate my little baby. Ben had gone - leaving me alone and numb.

It was a long time before the warm numbness began to fade and the real pain became apparent to me. For months I seemed to see-saw between living in my heart where I felt protected from the pain and living in my mind where all I could feel was the agony of my loss. And when the pain came I would cry for days on end tormented by thoughts of 'Why me?'

Slowly I began to notice that when I was in my heart I had thoughts like, 'Ben has really taught me a lot,' and 'How can I understand all this?' I realised then that when people stay locked in the mind - that is when the heart breaks.

I spent a lot of time observing the natural world because I found it very soothing. One day, while watching a flock of starlings flying past, I noticed one of them break away and fly off in the opposite direction. I remember thinking that he was like my little one, with somewhere else to go and something else to do. I had just started to understand, to accept and to feel grateful for what Ben's death had taught me and this was my turning point.

The crying began to change into deep sighing. Things were changing. My heart and mind had come into balance and a deep healing was taking place inside me. I felt the sweetness of acceptance replace the pain. I felt as if a bright, comforting light was entering into the darkness of my world, giving me clarity and hope for the future.

I began to wonder if perhaps my little son had only come to teach me something fundamentally important to my life. One thing was certain. I would never be the same again because the whole experience had changed me irreversibly - for the better. I had felt the pain of every mother who has ever lost a child and it had changed, refined and moulded me into someone else. I was left with a much deeper, more abiding compassion and understanding of how to help others through the grieving process.

I now see that nothing that happens to us is ever wasted. In fact, everything is a gift. My son gave me a small treasure which I will hold in my heart for eternity. He taught me never to turn away from the pain of life but instead to turn towards it with open arms and to welcome what it has to teach me. Pain need never be frightening to us if we truly understand its purpose in our lives.

'When the heart weeps for what it has lost, the spirit laughs for what it has found.'

Sufi aphorism

Life is often painful and this is a truth we simply cannot avoid. People we love may become ill and die, accidents can happen that rip away the fabric of our lives, as Sally discovered when her house was removed overnight by Hurricane Camille (page 74). These are things we have no control over. But what we do control is the way we choose to deal with what happens. A noble heart, the Buddhists say, is one that sheds its armour, opening itself fearlessly to both heartache and delight. Joan who is a dear friend could very easily have chosen to close down her heart and to feel embittered by the loss of her little son. Instead, his death became an enriching experience because she chose to see it in that way.

It is only possible to experience suffering as a gift if you are willing to look for and understand its deeper meaning and to resist the impulse to push it away. And those who are wise will always tell you to keep your heart open when it hurts.

It can often feel as if you have to accept situations as inevitable and out of your control, feeling powerless to influence a different course. But when you can approach life with the idea that you are not alone in any given situation you instantly become capable of reversing its potential. Any situation can be turned on its head, in fact, and given a new, energised perspective once we can recognise our intricate oneness with all things. It always helps to remember that everything in the universe is being perfectly guided by an unseen controller and that each situation is neither good nor bad. We are the ones who colour it with our own unique perspective, likes and dislikes.

The pain of life is something we all share, and have always shared. If you believe you have been singled out to have more than others you will find yourself contracting inside and this, as Joan said in her story, can break your heart. It's important to remember that everything passes and pain is only temporary. When you can embrace your suffering fearlessly, compassionately and with curiosity, as she did, you will discover the treasure hidden within it.

Q When was the last time you tried to avoid an unpleasant situation?

Q Can you think of any inner realisations that have come to you during or after a period of suffering and pain?

Q What positive situations are you in today that have arisen as a result of a painful episode in your life?

Turning

Point techniques

- Try this. Hold something you own personally for one minute. Say to yourself, 'This is not me or mine.'

- Next time you experience suffering go outside into nature, touch a leaf and stand still. Experience how the natural world dissolves pain away.

- Every day listen to the birds singing with all your attention for about thirty seconds. See how it enhances your ability to turn suffering into joy.

Your notes

Live with passion

'Whatever you can do, or dream you can, begin it. Boldness has genius, power and magic in it.'

Goethe

TURNING POINT - BARBARA

*A*s a fourteen year old girl I went to a grammar school in Berlin and, like most girls of my age, was preoccupied with how I looked, what people thought of me, the latest pop stars, new clothes and so on. One day our history teacher organised a special session for all the pupils of my year who were studying recent history and showed us some old film reels about the Third Reich. I could hardly believe what I saw. We had always been brought up to believe that the Russians had been the aggressors during the war and we were the innocent victims but here I was watching a film that told a very different story. It had been specially produced as a training film for SS personnel who worked in the extermination camps and showed in explicit and chilling detail how to deal with prisoners from the moment of their arrival until their end.

Sixty of us sat in shocked silence. About half left before the end. Many were sick there and then. When the film finished everyone else left the room without a word until I was the only one left. I sat rooted to the spot, unable to move and not knowing what to do. It was as though something inside me had turned to stone. I'm not sure how long I sat there until I could finally move. I didn't know who I could go to or talk to so I went outside. I looked up at the sky and asked the sun and the clouds to be my witness as I vowed to be one of the peacemakers of this world.

I changed dramatically overnight. My parents couldn't

understand what had happened to me because I suddenly set about investigating all kinds of youth organisations to see which were doing the most to help people in need and then threw myself wholeheartedly into their activities. I joined the Youth Community Service and helped with projects such as renovating old people's homes and shopping for old people. By the age of eighteen I had joined the adult branch and was soon working as a youth leader training other team leaders to work in the international work camps.

These projects brought volunteers together from all over the world and gave me the opportunity to work on reforestation projects and helping cancer patients in hospitals. I then went to Israel to work on a Kibbutz where I met a lot of Jewish people, some of whom could not face working with me because I was German. I shared accommodation with many Americans, Canadians and northern Europeans. We used to talk late into the night about the way forward for the world and discussed education as a means of helping people to understand each other without prejudice. Our heroes were people like Gandhi and Martin Luther King, whose famous speech 'I have a Dream' inspired me to adopt three mixed race children. I wanted to demonstrate that race, religion and caste do not have to separate people and that it doesn't matter what background people come from, love is the most important thing. We joined the human rights league and helped found a school for the education of gypsy children.

Now, in my fifties I am living in a community of people who have dedicated their lives to promoting peace worldwide. We organise international peace walks, so we can teach people self-help techniques for healing their painful emotions in places as diverse as Bosnia, Northern Ireland, Chechnya in Russia as well as Germany and Poland.

The pain I felt in my heart and mind on that fateful day in Berlin is still with me. I keep it alive so that I will not be able to forget my vow that I will not allow those people to have died in vain. Every day urges me on and reminds me that everything I do should be to create peace both inside and outside the individual. Many, many Germans of my generation have had an 'awakening' of this kind and it is that experience that has motivated them to work so hard for international peace and understanding.

'If a man does not keep pace with his companions, perhaps it is because he hears a different drummer. Let him step to the music which he hears, however measured and far away.'

Henry Thoreau

One of the greatest potential turning points occurs when we make the decision to turn away from the superficiality of life, when social chatter and behaviour starts to ring hollow in our ears and something inside is urging us on to create meaning in our existence. So much time and energy is depleted through excessive talking, empty socialising and trying to please the people around us. This is time and energy that could be channelled much more effectively into a passionate commitment for something we truly believe in.

People who live with passion will always achieve great things - people like Helen Keller, Mozart, Marie Curie, Abraham Lincoln, Martin Luther King, Gandhi, Mother Teresa, you - the list is endless. No doubt you could think of many more people yourself who made an impact through their commitment to what they really believed in. People who were really willing to make the effort to not just sit back and let life happen somehow or another.

Once you have a commitment it is amazing how people are attracted to being with you, because you are freer by knowing what you want for and from your life and are no longer willing to compromise in any way.

Having said that, it also often means you will have to walk alone. As Gandhi said, people are always ready to share the praise and the bounty with you but nobody wants to share your struggle and the effort it takes. That effort is discipline, patience and perseverance.

When Jesus entered Jerusalem on Palm Sunday everyone cheered and laid down palm leaves for him to ride over. By Good Friday no one wanted to follow him up the hill. Great leaders are able to walk on in the face of great prejudice and criticism which carves you out in the history of generations to come. When you have a passionate commitment to what you believe in, who you are lives on. You plant a tree that will give fruit to nourish generations to come and give them a real purpose in life.

Once we made the decision to take our self-help skills into war zones such as Bosnia where they are most needed, our lives have changed beyond our wildest dreams. This year we walked through the streets of Rotterdam with nearly 1000 people and then unveiled our Eurowalk peace pole in St. Jacobs Plaats. As hundreds of people gathered around the pole we laughed, cried and welcomed the sacred breeze together. It was almost as though a window had opened in the hearts of these people, bringing forth the power of their love. Later on in the day, 1500 people packed into a church together and I could tell from the look in their eyes that their lives had been changed by the experience. They had realised how much they could do to change their world.

Q What are you doing to set your heart on fire?

Q Are others inspired by your enthusiasm? Are you?

Q Do you ever watch the news and wish there was a way to help the trouble in the world?

Q Are you ever willing to 'simply start' to help the world?

Turning

Point techniques

- Find opportunities to do voluntary work in your local area.

- Read and learn skills about how to be a community peacemaker. Bringing laughter, healing or conflict resolution into your interactions is easier than you may think.

- The secret is to begin. Just start somewhere in earnest. Turn the news off and turn the *activity* on. Do something - anything - no matter how small to make somebody's life richer.

- Next time you see a thought provoking headline - stop! Turn off the TV or shut the newspaper. Sit down with a piece of paper and a pen and ask yourself deeply and sincerely in the quietest part of yourself - 'What can I do to help?' There is something - and the answer will come, even if it seems irrelevant. Write it down. Do it!

Let your life become filled with dozens of living
actions for peace. Soon you will find people are calling
you a peacemaker.

Your notes

Free
yourself

'The holiest spot on earth is where an
ancient hatred has become a present love.'

A Course in Miracles

*M*y relationship with my father had always been very much a love-hate relationship. Despite constant attempts by both of us to be reasonable and calm with each other it was practically impossible for us to enter into a discussion about anything without causing the rest of the family to run for shelter! This state of affairs continued until I was twenty-one.

One morning I was in the kitchen with my mother when Dad came downstairs looking green. We could tell at a glance that something was very wrong and he needed a doctor. My mother had to be at work that morning so I rushed him over to the surgery as quickly as I could. The doctor saw him almost straight away and I sat down to read magazines while I waited. Absorbed in the magazine articles I only gradually became aware that there was a lot of commotion going on around me and dimly picked out my name being called out above the noise. I went to the reception desk to discover that Dad had passed out in the surgery and had to be rushed to hospital. He had an ulcer and was losing a lot of blood internally.

Everything began to assume a dream-like quality as I followed him into the ambulance minutes later. Even when we arrived in hospital and he was connected up to lots of tubes it didn't really sink in how ill he was. It was only when the doctors explained that he had lost five pints of blood and that it was a miracle that he was still alive that it began to dawn on me that my parents wouldn't be around for ever. If either of them had died then I would certainly have lived with a lot of regrets because there was still so much to be sorted out between us. I resolved to do something about it straight away.

I did everything I could to care for Dad while he was in hospital and when he came home. None of the petty squabbles seemed significant any more. All that mattered was that Dad got better. Things seemed to be going much more smoothly between us so when Dad challenged me one day it came as a great shock. 'Do you realise you nearly killed me?' he shouted. 'All that arguing caused me such a lot of stress. That's what was responsible for the ulcer!' I was devastated. I couldn't bear to think that he really believed I had nearly killed him and neither could I afford to remain in a situation in which I might be even remotely responsible for creating problems for him. The only solution I could think of was to leave home.

I found a job selling health foods in a chemist's shop. This was perfect for me because I had recently begun to seriously investigate healthy diet and lifestyle programmes. There was a flat attached to the job and although I had nothing more than my sleeping bag and a fan heater to put in the room I didn't mind. I was very much into simple living so the whole arrangement suited me down to the ground. In the excitement of this new phase of discovery I didn't think too much about my resolve to build bridges within my family.

A conversation with a friend reminded me of it one day. It brought home to me that, although I had genuinely wanted to alleviate the situation at home by moving out, all I had succeeded in doing was to push it aside for a while. Nothing permanent had been resolved and I needed to make a serious effort to forgive past hurts and create a healing situation in the present. For the next two years I did everything in my power to let my parents know I loved them. I visited them, I phoned them, I sent them gifts and I made sure I said everything I needed to. There was no holding back.

Gradually I felt the rift healing and the connection between us becoming stronger. We started to discuss each other's opinions, our dreams and aspirations, and with this improved understanding we grew closer to each other. It took a lot of hard work and perseverance on both sides but it has paid off.

It was Dad's birthday a few weeks ago and I wanted to do something special for him. I got up at five o'clock in the morning so I could drive the hundred miles or so down the motorway to reach his office soon after he arrived at work. In I walked carrying a huge bunch of balloons to wish him a happy birthday. He was flabbergasted! He left his desk so we could talk for a while and I could tell he was happy and that he was proud of me. And I was proud of him.

It can take a lot of courage and hard work to forgive and build bridges but Dad and I have discovered that forgiveness is the most freeing thing in the world.

'An eye for an eye leaves the whole world blind.'

Gandhi

Have you ever noticed how people always remember the painful episodes of life in much more detail than the happy ones? And if someone says ten good things to you and one bad thing, you tend to remember the bad one? We also have a natural tendency towards blaming others for things that go wrong and this pattern of blame can be very hard to let go of once it is established in a relationship.

As a child I used to wrestle with my twin sister Rita. She loved to run into the room and jump on top of me when I was least expecting it. In seconds our arms and legs would become so intertwined that neither of us could escape. It didn't matter that she was the one who started the fight. It didn't really matter *who* started it because we both ended up trapped.

This is what it can be like in a relationship where both parties feel hurt and refuse to let go of the pain. Deliberately holding onto painful memories means that you both become ensnared and just as when I was wrestling with my sister, the only way out is for one person to decide to disentangle themselves. This is what forgiveness is all about. In the act of forgiving, all the thoughts and emotions that have been holding you down are suddenly released, leaving you free to continue with your life.

We know an amazing young girl from Holland called Anna. She was so concerned about the conflict she could see between the people around her that she decided to turn her fifteenth birthday into a 'Forgiveness Festival'. She sent out invitations to various relatives and friends who hadn't spoken to each other for years. Intrigued by the idea of a 'Forgiveness Festival' most of them turned up and were absolutely bowled over by the sincerity, wisdom and love of this young girl. She told them the true story of a young Jewish man who had become estranged from his father after a disagreement about their religion. He left home after a very heated argument and consequently broke all contact with his home and relations. He had no news of his family until many years later when he heard from a friend that his father had died.

He was completely grief stricken by the realisation that he would never have the chance to resolve his conflict with his father and the pain drove him back to Israel and the Jewish faith. He went straight to the Wailing Wall where, according to tradition, if you write your prayers on a piece of paper and leave them in a crack in the wall they will always be answered.

His only wish was that his father would forgive him for the

pain he had caused him and as he pushed his prayer into a tiny crevice, another piece of paper fell onto the ground. He couldn't resist reading it. It said, 'Son, if you ever by some miracle find this message I want you to know that I love you and I forgive you.' It was signed by his father!

The outcome of the Forgiveness Festival was astounding. Once people began to talk to each other openly they were able to understand that nobody ever deliberately hurts anyone else. We can only act to the best of our ability and to the best of our knowledge in the circumstances we find ourselves in. Long-standing rifts were healed and friendships were re-established. It is often said in ancient cultures that the process of forgiveness can liberate your greater source of compassion and wisdom.

When Eurowalk was in Northern Ireland the team met a minister who ran youth courses to help young people to heal their personal and inter-personal relationships. He told us about a community youth gathering in which everyone was asked to pray together and to share their prayers out loud if they felt the need. A young seventeen-year-old girl stood up and asked the group to pray for a man awaiting sentence in prison. Afterwards the minister asked her who the man was. 'He's the man who killed my father,' she said quietly, with no trace of anger or hatred.

In the end, it doesn't matter at all who is 'right' and who is 'wrong'. Forgiveness frees everyone.

Q Do you want to be right or do you want to be free?

Q Are you waiting for someone else to start the forgiveness process first?

Q Do you know people who easily forgive and those who don't? Can you feel the difference?

Q Have you had to forgive anyone recently? How did it feel?

- Follow Anna's example and start your own Forgiveness Revolution. Invite all your relatives who have unresolved issues to come and sort things out.

- Mentally see yourself apologising on a regular basis to the people you have hurt or are hurting at the moment. You will immediately see its impact on them. Once you are convinced that it's working at that subtle level, do something outwardly. For example you could send a letter, a card or a gift, and witness how it brings you closer together.

- One of the best ways to heal any relationship is to give a gift or a card on special occasions such as birthdays or Christmas. People love it. But don't just wait for special occasions. Give anyway, at any time.

- If someone has really hurt you:
  Let their words come into you as you breathe in and
  then breathe them out on the exhalation.

- Breathe the negativity in through your heart and out
  again through the crown of your head. Let God change
  it. Now breathe it back down through the top of your
  head and out of the heart into the person who has hurt
  you.

- Two excellent movement sequences to help heal pain
  are:
  *'The Letting Go sequence', which is described in
  Mansukh's book, 'Crisis and the Miracle of Love'.
  'Cutting the Illusion' which you will find on Mansukh's
  video tape 'Stepping Forward with Dru Yoga'.*

Your notes

Be still

Be still and know, both day and night
Be still and know, that dark and light
Are one holy circle.

Jokhim Meikle

TURNING POINT - SHEILA

I walked outside, instinctively looking up at the vast, silent night and from the depths of my anguish the words emerged, 'If there is anybody out there, please help me!' I had never really believed in the existence of a God but now, in my most desperate moment, and with no one else to turn to, I found myself praying. They say that in the fox holes of war there are no atheists...

But I was not involved in an external war. Mine was a war with myself and with my body. At forty-seven with children still young, I had just discovered that I had a fast growing form of breast cancer. And now I was being forced to face up to everything I had done that had contributed to it. Looking back I could see my lifestyle, though exciting, had not been a healthy one. After university I had travelled extensively, with many glamorous jobs, taken up dangerous sports and partied every night. I smoked and drank just about anything that came my way and moved from one relationship to another. My life was basically without direction but by keeping on the move constantly I could avoid the issue.

Cancer forced me to face the truth so that I could no longer ignore the inner darkness. The medical care I received was second to none, but I knew it wasn't enough and I was going to have to search for help of a different kind, although I had no idea what that would be.

And so I found myself appealing to the stars for help, reaching out to something much greater than anything I had previously known. And this was my turning point. The next day I met someone who introduced me to a retreat on Bardsey Island in North Wales and before I knew it, I had signed up for a week on a tiny island without electricity or hot water. Me! Who had never stopped still long enough to be with myself for fear of confronting the terrible void inside.

It turned out to be the happiest time I have ever experienced. The island is very sacred and elemental: 'a place where eternity meets time.' On Bardsey the sun seems brighter, the rain purer and the wind wilder than anywhere else. Wherever you are you can always hear the sea pounding the rocky coast. As a group we walked in sunshine and rain, ate, sang and laughed together and in the sanctuary of the beautiful little chapel we learned to meditate. For the first time in my life I felt *safe*.

I had never done yoga or meditation before, but by the time I left the island I was committed to getting up early before my family to do both. As I started to slow down and to become still inside, I also began to get to know myself and to my amazement to like what I found.

Seven years on I wake up each morning full of gratitude that I am alive and well and excited about what the day will bring. My life now feels very full and I have never felt happier. My prayer was answered in the most unexpected way.

'Stillness, silence and solitude are necessary to come to the awareness of who we are.'

Do you ever long to feel peaceful, united, harmonized and a part of everything, instead of out of rhythm and out of tune with everything and everyone around you?

People are always asking me what it is that gives me the energy, enthusiasm, peace of mind and mental balance I need to deal with my very demanding lifestyle, and I always say quite categorically that it is sitting quietly every day sometimes for many hours, just being with myself. Silence, I have found, is one of the most powerful friends you can have in life. It creates a firm foundation on which to build your daily experiences.

The hunger to feel complete and to belong lies at the very heart of our human nature and the day you decide to sit with yourself in silence will be the day you create one of the most important turning points in your life. Even a few minutes a day can make a significant difference to your whole experience and perspective on life: your work, relationships at work and home as well as your inner emotional environment.

People often say they cannot afford to spend time in solitude and contemplation, but I always say, 'Can you afford not to?'

Out of the 1,440 minutes in your day, can you not find twenty minutes to transform your life? People like Einstein, Gandhi, Jesus and many others chose to spend many hours in silence or out in nature. As a result they often had to endure a lot of criticism from friends and families who couldn't understand their need for solitude. I think it is true to say that it is this quality time spent alone that has produced the greatest masterpieces that continue to endure to this day.

I love walking on my own for hours on end. In fact, some of my most creative and explosive insights have come to me while on the road walking alone. These ideas, when crystallized and applied, have the potential to help a lot of people.

Sitting quietly and focusing the mind for a few minutes is like turning over a new leaf - to find a fresh one you didn't even know existed before. Try it!

Q How much time do you spend in solitude?

Q Do you try to feel peaceful, united, harmonised and a part of everything?

Q What price do you personally pay for not taking time out to be still?

Turning

Point techniques

- The next time you sit still, perhaps in a pause between sips of tea, listen to the beat of your heart. Notice the flow of your breath and the colours around you.

- Put aside 5-10 minutes every day first thing in the morning before you jump out of bed. Notice the sensations in your body. Feel your breath. Smile.

- Imagine you are in a lift and as you count to ten you are going down ten floors. The doors open and you walk into a room with a sofa in it. Lie down on the sofa and have a rest for a few minutes. Then get back into the lift and count from ten to one as you rise up again.

- Practise this simple mediatation technique for a few minutes every day, preferably first thing in the morning and/or just before you go to bed.
  Give yourself a good stretch to release any physical tension.

Sit down somewhere where you will not be disturbed for five to ten minutes. Keep your back straight, breathe in deeply and as you exhale allow your body to relax. Relax your legs, then your abdomen, your chest, your arms and finally your face and head.

Feel your breath as it enters your nostrils and as it leaves again. That's all you have to do! If your mind wants to think of other things at the same time, ask the other thoughts to go away for the time being so you can focus all your attention on watching your breath as it enters and leaves your body.

When you feel ready to come out of the meditation, cover your face with your hands, open your eyes and slowly slide your hands away. Rest for a few moments before moving.

Your notes

Go deeper

'Who looks outside dreams; who looks
inwards wakes.'

Carl Jung

TURNING POINT - MARIANNE

When you crash head-on into a dyke wall at 70 kilometres per hour you know your life is never going to be the same again. I did attempt for a short while to pretend everything was normal as I tried to reassure my children in the back of the car, but my next conscious memory is of waking up in the intensive care unit with fourteen fractures. My pelvis was in three pieces and every limb of my body was damaged. My temperature climbed above 42 degrees – higher than the top reading on the hospital thermometer. The pain and fear I felt were indescribable. I remember having problems with my breathing and finding myself hovering above my bed, looking down at my body and all its tubes. Thinking about it later, I guess this was a near-death experience, and I felt peace for the first time. Freedom from pain!

Yet I also felt great panic that I would be without my children. I didn't want to go.

Despite the severity of the injuries, my body healed at an astonishing rate. I was out of intensive care after ten days, home in two and a half weeks and walking in three weeks. Soon after returning home, however I found myself in such pain from the fractures that I once again left my body. All I can say is that I knew I was with God. Waves of peace and a deep, solid, accepting love washed all around me as He spoke to me and told me very gently and lovingly but very firmly that I couldn't keep on doing this. I still had responsibilities to fulfil in the world. I had to come back.

But this time I knew I had found something I had been seeking for years before the accident. I had been exploring the world of spirituality and went to a meditation class at my local church. But the accident had clearly shown me that what I had been doing hadn't been enough. When I had really been put to the test all I had experienced was pain and fear – not the peace and trust that I had hoped would be there. In a strange way I began to feel grateful that my injuries had been so severe because I knew that if I had only had one broken bone it wouldn't have been enough to make me stop and think more seriously.

I went on courses and retreats and learned to meditate in a deeper way. I also learned what it meant to really pray. Miraculously, my husband, whose interest in such things had been very superficial before, joined me. We soaked up everything we could find and were much better able to meet the challenges when our next big test hit us.

We were at home one afternoon when I began to get a very uneasy feeling about my eight-year-old son who was out playing on my neighbour's farm. We rushed over and arrived to discover that he had just fallen from the top of a four metre high haystack and landed on his head. He was rushed to hospital with a broken skull. For four days he was in a coma and it was touch and go whether or not he would survive. That first day was very hard because we were only allowed in to see him once every hour. But we hung on to what we had learned about prayer and meditation and I'm convinced that that is what saw us through.

In fact the days and weeks following Johan's fall were very peaceful in many ways. We didn't know at first if there would be any permanent brain damage, or if he would recover at all, but even so there was a sense of completeness - a total acceptance of life as it is. Sitting with him day and night, in prayer and meditation, we realised just what is possible. As soon as you are helping someone else you tap into another source of energy that is limitless. In many ways it was quite a miraculous time for us. Even if Johan had died and we'd had to face the grief of losing him, that still couldn't have taken away the feelings of love and peace that had surrounded us during those ten days of sitting with him. I felt supported and in control. I even went to Johan's school one day and talked to the other children in his class about what was happening to him.

In hospital my husband and I would sit at either side of Johan's bed and hold his hands. At first it felt as if he was just floating but then came the magical moment when we felt he had started to fight. You could see the effect our presence had on him from the monitors. Sometimes we had to leave him while the nurses treated him but as soon as we were by his side again, holding his hands and meditating, his heart rhythm would immediately slow down and he would become peaceful once more. It was magical to experience life in this way.

Johan regained consciousness after four days. It was a very deep experience for me. It really felt like a second birth. Our eyes met and we recognised each other and knew that everything would be all right.

Those first few days with him were very precious, and very subtle. It had been a real test of surrender but I knew I had found what I had been looking for after my own accident. Once Johan came out of intensive care he improved quickly and was soon running around the wards looking for someone to play football with him. He came out of hospital two and a half weeks later and made a full recovery. It was not long before I looked out of my window to see him climbing trees. But I wasn't afraid for him. I had learned to trust that he would be looked after and I felt happy to see him free.

'The rung of a ladder was never meant to rest upon but only to hold a man's foot long enough to enable him to put the other somewhat higher.'

Thomas Henry Huxley

It can be very exciting when you first start to explore spiritual life and you realise that you can be in control of your thoughts and emotions. Your meditation practice brings you a sense of peace and contentment and you suddenly find yourself able to ride the storms of life with unexpected ease. Life seems very rosy until, out of the blue, you may be confronted with a major challenge that throws you off balance and then you realise that your firm foundation of peace isn't quite as firm as you thought it was.

Our Snowdon Lodge course centre is surrounded by mountains and whenever I get the chance I like to take time out from a busy teaching schedule to climb one of them. If you climb just a little way up you get to see a certain amount of the landscape, but the higher you climb the more the view expands. And if you want to see more you have to climb even higher. This is what spirituality is like. You can sit comfortably on the foothills of the spiritual mountain for years, but if you really want to go deeper into life's mystery you simply have to put more into it.

Years ago, Mansukh's mother told me a story which beautifully illustrates this need to keep going deeper in order to reap the rewards of your spiritual practice.

There once was a poor woodcutter who lived in a small hut at the edge of a forest. Every day he walked a short distance into the forest, cut down a tree and took it to market to sell. In this way he worked extremely hard to eke out a meagre living but barely had enough to feed his family. One day he met a wise, old man and told him his troubles. 'You have to go deeper into the wood,' said the sage. So the next day the woodcutter walked further into the forest where he found groves of much rarer trees that brought him a better price at the market. This then became his regular working ground.

Some time later he met the same sage again. 'How are you getting on now, my friend?' the sage asked. 'Much better,' replied the woodcutter. 'I have more food now but it's still very hard work cutting trees and going to the market every day.' 'Go deeper into the wood,' advised the sage. So the woodcutter made his way towards the heart of the forest. There he discovered the rarest and most beautiful trees of all. In taking just one of these trees to market he was able to earn enough money to support his family for many weeks. His life became easier and more fulfilling and he had enough to see him through the hard times without having to worry.

TURNING POINT - MARIANNE

Q What is more important to you, the journey or the destination?

Q Are you content just knowing half the truth or would you like to go deeper into life's mystery?

Q Have you ever noticed that some of the most successful and creative people in this world are those who go beyond the normal boundaries of life? Which boundaries are you prepared to break now?

Q Think of an area of your life in which you feel content. You are resting on a rung of your ladder. What do you need to do to get up to the next rung?

Turning

Point techniques

- Take one simple activity in your life and think about three ways in which to make it more exciting and meaningful and of wider application.

- Take a few moments every day to focus on one person within your family circle and observe the way they operate. Notice their laughter, their behaviour and their expressions, and at the end of that brief period observe how much deeper your appreciation is of that person. If you have nobody around you, then start with yourself. Or watch the goldfish or budgie!

- Pick up something that belongs to you and has a deep personal significance. Reach into its memories. See how it awakens respect and reverence for life within you.

Turning Point

Your Turning Point

Do you have a turning point story which you think could help other people? If you would like to share it and would be happy for us to print it in a future book, please contact us at: Life Foundation Publications, Maristowe House, Dover Street, Bilston, West Midlands, WV14 6AL, UK

FACE TO FACE WITH LIFE

Dr Mansukh Patel and John Jones

'Face to Face with Life' is a powerful handbook for successful living...it is also a miraculous true story. It contains over a hundred breakthrough techniques to increase self-esteem, improve relationships and develop inner calm. Meanwhile, enjoy the gripping story of a group of University students who became the pioneers of the Life Foundation, and who have brought real happiness into thousands of lives world-wide.

This popular book is now available in Dutch from Ankh Hermes.

THE DANCE BETWEEN JOY AND PAIN

Dr Mansukh Patel & Rita Goswami

This handbook has become a source of inspiration and reference for thousands of people since it was first published in 1995. It is a manual for mastering all the

negative emotions we experience, from anger and grief to jealousy and loneliness. Practical movements, breathing exercises and hand gestures combine to transform emotions into positive tools to enrich every aspect of life. *Now in it's fifth reprint, The Dance Between Joy and Pain is available in Dutch, French and German.*

CRISIS AND THE MIRACLE OF LOVE

Dr Mansukh Patel and Dr Helena Waters

At every stage of life there is a point of power, a time when an intense amount of energy is made available to us for our emotional and spiritual growth. These pockets of energy contain immense creative potential that can be effectively harnessed to accelerate our success in life. Read how to turn your crises into opportunities, access your creative potential, create successful and lasting relationships, work with your children and understand the process and real meaning of death. This excellent book contains over 35 techniques and action plans and the brilliant Golden Triangle programme.

YOUR PERSONAL PEACE FORMULA

Dr Mansukh Patel

The Peace Formula offers fascinating new perspectives which enable us to accomplish our highest dreams and ideals. This simple Seven Point Plan has been tried and tested by some of the greatest people of our time like Mahatma Gandhi, Martin Luther King, Mother Teresa and many others. It has the power to create lasting inner change that will ripple out into every aspect of your life - and beyond.

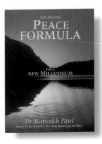

WALKING WITH THE BHAGAVAD GITA - VOL. 1 (CHAPT 1- 6)

Savitri MacCuish, Dr Mansukh Patel and John Jones
'Bhagavad Gita' can be translated from the original Sanskrit as 'The Song of the Lord'. It is one of the oldest scriptural texts known to man, first set down centuries before the birth of Christ. It is the ultimate handbook for learning how to design your life, containing the essence of everything you need to know in order to discover your true nature and purpose in life.

In this beautiful book, Mansukh Patel magnificently describes the dialogue between Lord Krishna and Arjuna, followed by an inspired commentary by Savitri MacCuish and John Jones. Also included are daily meditations and exercises, exquisite illustrations, the original Sanskrit text in Devanagari script, as well as a guide to the characters, a Sanskrit pronunciation guide, glossary and advice on how to chant the Gita slokas.

THE BHAGAVAD GITA VIDEO SERIES

narrated by Dr Mansukh Patel
In this series of stunning documentaries, one for each chapter of the Bhagavad Gita, Mansukh's original insights into its message are illustrated by fascinating anecdotes from his own life and his experiences on Eurowalk 2000. Mansukh also demonstrates flowing Dru Yoga movements to complement the Gita's message.

STEPPING FORWARD

Dr Mansukh Patel, Jane Patel and Annie Jones
This video includes:
1. Seven part activation
2. Eight part Body Tone
3. sequences - Earth sequence (removes rigidity through dynamic creative movements), Salutations to the Vision of Truth, Cutting the Illusion (releases fear and activates the heart)
4. Mudras (directs, focus and contain your energy)
5. Meditation (works on endocrine and and nervous systems)

186

INSOMNIA
Anita Goswami

Say goodnight to insomnia! There is a wealth of natural remedies and techniques available to guarantee a good night's sleep. On this informative tape, Anita reveals the causes and solutions to insomnia. Ideal to use just before bed, this cassette includes tips for a good night's sleep and a soothing and sleep-promoting guided relaxation.

ENERGY BLOCK RELEASE 3 & 4
Anita Goswami & Regina Doerstel

Energy Block Release (EBR) 3 is entitled 'Awakening the Heart' and includes fourteen graceful movements which bring a profound sense of harmony. On side B of the tape, enjoy the 'Mudra Energisation Sequence' (EBR 4), which uses hand postures to intensify the powerful balancing effects of the movements. The benefits of these sequences include improved communication, postural alignment and physical and emotional balance.

ENERGY BLOCK RELEASE 5 & 6
Anita Goswami & Sian Edwards

This tape contains two energy block release movement sequences (EBR) which are designed to enhance your natural energy. EBR 5 creates a natural flow and rhythm enabling you to let go of deep emotional patterns so you can clearly see your goals in life. EBR 6 is designed to activate and empower the energy of the heart. Learn how to open your heart and lungs, improve your body-mind co-ordination and banish depression, sadness and grief. These original Dru Yoga sequences are ideal for anyone who wants to explore the richness and depth of this graceful art.

DEEP RELAXATION
Anita Goswami

Side A of this tape invites you to sit back and unwind with a short relaxation in a chair, ideal for the office or at home. The second side contains a longer guided relaxation with harmonious background music making it the ideal tonic for life's stresses and strains.

Courses

INTERNATIONAL LIFE CONFERENCE

The Life Conference is the heart-filled event of the year! Come and experience a new way of looking at life which will give you the tools to heal yourself. Packed with workshops entertainment and oustanding speakers, we also offer delicious vegetarian cuisine and a full youth programme.

SNOWDON LODGE INTERNATIONAL RETREAT CENTRE - NORTH WALES

Snowdon Lodge lies in the spectacular Nant Ffrancon Valley, the heart of Snowdonia, set amidst glorious countryside. Everything about Snowdon Lodge is designed to put you at ease, helping you to shed the stress of a busy life, worlds away from city bustle and work schedules.

Full facilities of Snowdon Lodge are also available for hire on a daily or residential basis, providing an ideal setting for business meetings, management training, seminars and workshops, leisure and health groups. Use your own tutors or take advantage of our experts who can help you design a programme to suit the special needs of your group.

Accommodation provides a spectacular view of the Snowdonia mountains, while the fresh, tempting vegetarian cuisine (including special dietary requirements) is also available in our Welsh restaurant. Our on-site shop carries an excellent collection of self-development books, tapes and videos as well as gifts and snacks.

courses include:

Bhagavad Gita Retreats, Dru Yoga Open retreats, Heart Vipassana Meditation Retreat, Pathfinders, Tai Chi and Chi Kung, Vital Nutrition for Health, Women's Health Matters.

DRU YOGA THERAPY TRAINING COURSE

More than 240 students have successfully completed the Dru Yoga Therapy course over the last eight years. Our tutors are well respected, vesatile and creative. There are Dru Yoga tutors in the USA, Australia, Germany, Netherlands, Ireland and the UK. Dru Yoga therapists are able to use their integrated approach to yoga in hospitals, LEA classes, prisons, sports centres, international conferences and a wide variety of life settings..the list is endless.

BARDSEY ISLAND RETREATS

Imagine getting away from it all - no cars, shops, computers, electricity or phones...Bardsey Island is simply idyllic. Rediscover the magic of your own inner peace, enjoy home cooking and make new friends. Bardsey is an unspoilt, magical island at the end of the Llŷn Peninsula, North Wales and has been known as a holy island since the 5th century.

LIFE YOUTH PROJECTS

This scheme seeks to sponsor outstanding young people from every continent of the world, to join LFST's youth events and engage in a programme of self discovery and empowerment.

Please send for our free colour brochure available from Snowdon Lodge (see page 189)

USEFUL ADDRESSES

The Life Foundation School of Therapeutics has established the following permenant bases:

Life Foundation School of Therapeutics (UK)
Registered Office
Maristowe House, Dover Street, West Midlands WV14 6AL
Tel: +44 (0)1902 409164
Fax: +44 (0)1902 497362
E-mail - info@lifefoundation.org.uk

Life Foundation School of Therapeutics (UK)
Snowdon Lodge - International Training Centre
Nant Ffrancon, Ty'n y Maes, Bethesda, Gwynedd LL57 3LX
Tel: +44 (0)1248 602900
Fax: +44 (0)1248 602004
E-mail - snowdonlodge@lifefoundation.org.uk

Life Foundation School of Therapeutics, USA
5004 Sunsuite Trail South, Colorado Springs, CO 80917, USA
Tel: 719 574 5452
Fax: 719 597 7929
E-mail - reggiedoe@aol.com

Life Foundation School of Therapeutics (Netherlands)
Postbus 88, 6670 AB ZETTEN, The Netherlands
Tel: 488 491387
Fax: 488 491545
E-mail - LFSTnether@aol.com

Life Foundation School of Therapeutics (Australia) Ltd
PO Box 543, Southport BC, Queensland 4215, Australia
E-mail - Lifeaus@aol.com

There are also full-time LFST representatives in the following areas:
Germany, London, Newcastle, Northern Ireland and Scotland, .

For details of events in these areas please contact: The Outreach Director, Life Foundation School of Therapeutics (UK), Snowdon Lodge (see above).

O Great Spirit
whose voice I hear in the winds,
And whose breath gives life to all the world,
Hear me!
Let me walk in beauty and make my eyes
Ever behold the red and purple sunset.
Make my hands respect the things you have made
And my ears sharp to hear your voice.
Let me learn the lessons you have hidden
in every leaf and rock.
I seek strength, not to be greater than my brother,
But to fight my greatest enemy
– myself.
Make me always ready to come to you
with clean hands and straight eyes,
So when life fades, as the fading sunset,
My spirit may come to you without shame.

Native American Prayer